The Practice of Piety

The Practice of Piety

A Puritan devotional manual,
directing a Christian how to live,
that he may please God

By

Lewis Bayly

Bottom of the Hill Publishing
Memphis, TN
www.BottomoftheHillPublishing.com

ISBN: 978-1-61203-833-9

Content

MEDITATIONS ON THE MISERABLE STATE OF THOSE NOT RECONCILED TO GOD IN CHRIST

O wretched man! Where shall I begin to describe your endless misery, who are condemned as soon as conceived; and judged to eternal death, before you were born to a temporal life! A beginning indeed, I find—but no end of your miseries. For when Adam and Eve, being created after God's own image, and placed in Paradise, that they and their posterity might live in a blessed state of life immortal, having dominion over all earthly creatures, and only restrained from the fruit of one tree, as a sign of their subjection to the almighty Creator; though God forbade them this one small thing, under the penalty of eternal death; yet they believed the devil's word before the word of God, making God, as much as in them lay, a liar. And so being unthankful for all the benefits which God bestowed on them, they became malcontent with their present state, as if God had dealt enviously or niggardly with them; and believed that the devil would make them partakers of far more glorious things than ever God had bestowed upon them; and in their pride they fell into high-treason against the Most High; and disdaining to be God's subjects, they attempted blasphemously to be gods themselves, equals to God. Hence, until they repented they became like the devil; and so all their posterity, as a traitorous brood (while they remain impenitent, like you) and are subject in this life to all cursed miseries, and, in the life to come, to the everlasting fire prepared for the devil and his angels.

Lay then aside for a while your doting vanities, and take the view with me of your doleful miseries; which duly surveyed, I doubt not but that you will conclude, that it is far better never to have been born, than not to be by grace, a practitioner of religious piety.

Consider therefore your misery:

1. In your life.
2. In your death.
3. After death.

In your **life**, 1. The miseries accompanying your body; 2. The miseries which deform your soul.

In your **death**, The miseries which shall oppress your body and soul.

After death, The miseries which overwhelm both body and soul together in hell.

I. Miseries in this PRESENT LIFE.

A. The miseries of the BODY from infancy to old age.

And, first, let us take a view of those miseries which accompany the body in the four ages of life, namely infancy, youth, adulthood, and old age.

1. What were you, being an **INFANT**—but an helpless unconscious creature, having the human form—but without speech or reason? You were born with the stain of original sin, and cast naked upon the earth. What cause then have you to boast of your birth, which was pain and anguish to your mother, and to yourself the entrance into a troublesome life? The greatness of which miseries, because you could not utter in words, you did express as well as you could in weeping tears!

2. What is **YOUTH**—but an untamed beast? All whose actions are rash and crude, not capable of good counsel, when it is given; and, ape-like, delighting in nothing but in toys and baubles? Therefore you no sooner began to have a little strength and discretion—but immediately you were kept under the rod, and fear of parents and masters; as if you had been born to live under the discipline of others, rather than at the disposition of your own will. No tired horse was ever more willing to be rid of his burden, than you were to get out of the servile state of this bondage—a state not worth the description.

3. What is **ADULTHOOD** but a sea, wherein, as waves, one trouble arises on the crest of another—the latter worse than the former? No sooner did you enter into the affairs of this world—but you were enwrapped about with a cloud of miseries. Your **flesh** provokes you to lust, the **world** allures you to pleasures, and the **devil** tempts you to all kinds of sins; fears of enemies affright you; lawsuits vex you; wrongs of bad neighbors oppress you; cares for wife and children consume you; and disquietness from open foes and false friends do in a manner confound you; sin stings you within; Satan lays snares before you; conscience of past sins, dog behind you.

Now **adversity** on the left hand frets you; anon, prosperity on your right hand flatters you! Over your head God's vengeance due to your sin is ready to fall upon you; and under your feet, hell's mouth is ready to swallow you up! **And in this miserable estate, where will you go for rest and comfort?** The house is full of cares, the field is full of toil, the country is full of crudeness, the city is full of factions, the court is full of envy, the church is full of sects, the sea is full of pirates, the land is full of robbers. Or in what state will you live, seeing wealth is envied—and poverty despised; wit is distrusted—and simplicity is derided; superstition is mocked—and religion is suspected; vice is advanced—and virtue is disgraced?

Oh, with what a body of sin are you compassed about, in this world of wickedness! What are your **eyes**—but windows to behold vanities? What are your **ears**—but flood-gates to let in the streams of iniquity? What are your **senses**—but matches to give fire to your lusts? What is your **heart**—but the anvil whereon Satan has forged the ugly shape of all lewd affections?

Are you **nobly** descended? You must put yourself in peril of foreign wars to get the reputation of earthly honor; oft-times hazard your life in a desperate combat to avoid the aspersion of a coward. Are you born in **poverty**? What pains and drudgery must you endure at home and abroad to get maintenance; and all perhaps scarcely sufficient to serve your necessity. And when, after much service and labor, a man has got something, how little certainty is there in that which is gotten? You see in daily experience, that he who was rich yesterday, is today a beggar; he that yesterday was in health, today is sick; he that yesterday was merry and laughing, has cause today to mourn and weep; he that yesterday was in favor, today is in disgrace; and he who yesterday was alive, today is dead! And you know not how soon, nor in what manner you shall die yourself! And **who can enumerate the losses, crosses, griefs, disgraces, sicknesses, and calamities, which are incident to sinful man?** To speak nothing of the death of friends and children, which oft-times seems to us far more bitter than present death itself.

4. What is **OLD AGE**—but the receptacle of all maladies? For if your lot be to draw your days to a long date, in comes old bald-headed age, stooping under dotage, with his wrinkled face, decaying teeth, and offensive breath; testy with irritability, withered with dryness, dimmed with blindness, obscured with deafness, overwhelmed with sickness, and bowed together with weakness; having no use of any sense—but of the sense of pain, which so racks every member of his body, that it never eases him of grief, until it has thrown him down to his grave.

Thus far of the miseries which accompany the body. Now of the miseries which accompany chiefly the soul in this life.

B. The miseries of the SOUL from infancy to old age.

The misery of your soul will more evidently appear, if you will but consider—

The felicity she has lost.

The misery which she has brought upon herself by sin.

1. The felicity the soul has LOST was,

First, the fruition of the image of God, whereby the soul was like God in knowledge, enabling her perfectly to understand the revealed will of God (Col. 3:10; Rom. 12:2)

Secondly, true holiness, by which she was free from all profane error.

Thirdly, righteousness, whereby she was able to incline all her natural powers. And to frame uprightly all her actions, proceeding from those powers. With the loss of this divine image, she lost the love of God, and the blessed communion which she had with Him, wherein consists her life and happiness. If the loss of earthly riches vex you so much, how should not the loss of this divine treasure perplex you much more?

2. The misery which the soul has brought upon herself by sin, consists in two things:

Sinfulness

Cursedness

1. SINFULNESS is an universal corruption both of the soul's nature and actions. The soul's nature is infected with a proneness to every sin continually (Eph. 2:3; Gen. 6:5). The **mind** is stuffed with vanity (Rom. 12:2; Eph. 4:17). The **understanding** is darkened with ignorance (1 Cor. 2:14). The **will** affects nothing but vile and vain things (Phil. 2:3). The soul's **actions** are evil (Rom. 3:12). Yes, this deformity is so violent, that often in the regenerate soul, the appetite will not obey the government of reason, and the will wanders after, and yields consent to sinful motions. How great, then, is the violence of the appetite and will in the reprobate soul, which still remains in her natural corruption! Hence it is that your wretched soul is so deformed with sin, defiled with lust, polluted with filthiness, outraged with passions, overgrown with vile affections, pining with envy, overcharged with gluttony, surfeited with drunkenness, boiling with revenge, transported with rage—and the glorious image of God transformed into the ugly shape of the devil (Jn. 8:44)—so far as it once "repented the Lord, that ever he made man!" Gen. 6:6.

2. From the former flows the other part of the soul's miseries, called **CURSEDNESS** (Dt. 27:26; Gal. 3:10; Ps. 119:21); whereof there are two degrees:

in part

in the fullness thereof

1. Cursedness in PART is that which is inflicted upon the soul in life and death, and is common to her with the body.

2. The cursedness of the soul in life, is the wrath of God, which lies upon such a creature so far, as that all things, not only calamities—but also very blessings and graces turn to ruin (Rom. 2:4,5; Jer. 28:13; Isa. 28:13); terror of conscience drives him from God and his service, that he dares not come to his presence and ordinances (Gen. 3:8,10; 4:14; Heb. 2:15)—but is given up to the slavery of Satan, and to his own lusts and vile affections (Rom. 1:21, 24, 26; Eph. 2:2; Col. 1:13). This is the cursedness of the soul in life. Now follow the cursedness of the soul and body in death.

II. The Misery of the body and soul in DEATH.

After that the aged man has battled with long sickness, and having endured the brunt of pain, and now expect some ease—in comes death, nature's slaughter-man, God's curse, and hell's supplier—and looks the old man grim and black in the face; and neither pitying his age, nor regarding his long-endured dolours, will not be hired to refrain either for silver or gold; nay, he will not take to spare his life, skin for skin (Job 1), and all that the old man has! But death batters all the principal parts of his body, and arrests him to appear before the dreadful Judge. And as thinking that the old man will not dispatch to go with him fast enough, Lord!—how many darts of calamities does he shoot through him—pains, aches, cramps, fevers, obstructions, weak heart, shortness of breath, colic, stone, etc. Oh, what a ghastly sight it is, to see him then in his bed, when death has given him his mortal wound! What a cold sweat over-runs all his body—what a trembling possesses all his members! The head hangs limp, the face waxes pale, the nose purples, the jaw-bone hangs down, the eye-strings break, the tongue falters, the breath shortens and smells foul, and at every gasp the heart-strings are ready to break asunder!

Now the miserable soul sensibly perceives her earthly body to begin to die; for as towards the dissolution of the universal frame of the great world, the sun shall be turned into darkness, the moon into blood, and the stars shall fall from heaven, the air shall be full of storms and flashing meteors, the earth shall tremble, and the sea shall roar, and men's hearts shall fail for fear, expecting the end of such sorrowful beginnings; in like manner, towards the dissolution of man, which is his little world, his eyes, which are as the sun and moon, lose their light, and see nothing but blood-guiltiness of sin; the rest of the senses, as lesser stars, do one after another fail and fall—his mind, reason, and memory, as heavenly powers of his soul, are shaken with fearful storms of despair, and fierce flashings of hell fire—his earthly body begins to shake and tremble, and the phlegm, like an overflowing sea, roar and rattle in his throat, still expecting the woeful end of these dreadful beginnings.

While he is thus summoned to appear at the great assizes of God's judgment, behold, a quarter-sessions and jail-delivery is held within himself; where reason sits as judge, the devil puts in a bill of indictment, wherein is alleged all your evil deeds that ever you have committed, and all the good deeds that ever you have omitted, and all the curses and judgments that are due to every sin. Your own conscience shall accuse you, and your memory shall give bitter evidence, and death stands at the bar ready, as a cruel executioner, to dispatch you. If you shall thus condemn yourself, how shall you escape the just condemnation of God, who knows all your misdeeds better than yourself? (1 Jn. 3:20) Gladly would you put out of your mind the remembrance of your wicked deeds that trouble you; but they flow faster into your remembrance, and they will not be put away, but cry unto you—We are your works, and we will follow you!

And while your soul is thus within, out of peace and order, your children, wife, and friends trouble you as fast, to have you put your goods in order; some crying, some craving, some pitying, some cheering; all, like flesh-flies, helping to make your sorrows more sorrowful (Lk. 12:20). Now the devils, who are come from hell to fetch away your soul, begin to appear to her; and wait, as soon as she comes forth, to take her, and carry her away. Your soul would like to stay within—but that she feels the body begin by degrees to die, and ready, like a ruinous house, to fall upon her head. Fearful she is to come forth, because of those hell-hounds which wait for her coming.

Oh, she that spent so many days and nights in vain and idle pastimes, would now give the whole world, if she had it, for one hour's delay, that she might have space to repent, and reconcile herself unto God! But it cannot be, because her body, which joined with her in the actions of sin, is altogether now unfit to join with her in the exercise of repentance—and repentance must be of the whole man.

Now she sees that all her pleasures are gone, as if they had never been; and that but only torments remain, which never shall have an end of being. Who can sufficiently express her remorse for her sins past, her anguish for her present misery, and her terror for her torments to come?

In this extremity she looks everywhere for help, and she finds herself every way helpless. Thus in her greatest misery, desirous to hear the least word of comfort, she directs this or the like speech to her **eyes**—O eyes, who in times past were so quick-sighted, can you spy no comfort, nor any way how I might escape this dreadful danger? But the eye-strings are broken, they cannot see the candle that burns before them, nor discern whether it is day or night.

The soul, finding no comfort in the eyes, speaks to the ears—O **ears**, who were accustomed to recreate yourselves with hearing new pleasant discourses, and music's sweetest harmony, can you hear any news or tidings of the least comfort for me? The ears are either so deaf, that they cannot hear at all, or the sense of hearing is grown so weak, that it cannot endure to hear his dearest friends speak. And why should those ears hear any tidings of joy in death, who could never abide to hear the glad tidings of the gospel in this life? The ear can minister no comfort.

Then she intimates her grief to the **tongue**—O tongue, who were accustomed to brag it out with the bravest, where are now your big and daring words? Now, in my greatest need, Can you speak nothing in my defense? Can you neither daunt these enemies with threatening words, nor entreat them with fair speeches? Alas! the tongue two days ago lay speechless—it cannot, in his greatest extremity, either call for a little drink, or desire a friend to take away with his finger the phlegm that is ready to choke him.

Finding here no hope of help, she speaks to the **feet**—Where are you, O feet, which once were so nimble in running? Can you carry me nowhere out of this dangerous place? The feet are stone-dead already—if they be not stirred, they cannot stir.

Then she directs her speech to her **hands**—O hands, who have been so often approved for manhood, in peace and war, and wherewith I have so often defended myself, and conquered my foes, never had I more need than now. Death looks me grim in the face, and kills me—hellish fiends wait about my bed to devour me—help now, or I perish forever. Alas! the hands are so weak, and do so tremble, that they cannot reach to the mouth a spoonful of liquid, to relieve languishing nature.

The wretched soul, seeing herself thus desolate, and altogether destitute of friends, help, and comfort, and knowing that within an hour she must be in everlasting pains, retires herself to the **heart** (which of all members is prime faculty), from whence she makes this doleful lamentation with herself.

O miserable coward that I am! How do the sorrows of death encompass me! How do the floods of Belial make me afraid! (2 Sam. 22:5) Now have, indeed, the snares both of the first and second death overtaken me at once. O how suddenly has death stolen upon me with insensible degrees! Like the sun, which the eye perceives not to move, though it be most swift of motion. How does death wreak on me his spite without pity! The God of mercy has utterly forsaken me; and the devil, who knows no mercy, waits to take me! How often have I been warned of this doleful day by the faithful preachers of God's word, and I made but a jest of it! What profit have I now of all my pride, fine house, and mirthful apparel? What is become of the sweet relish of all my delicious foods? All the worldly goods which I so carefully gathered, would I now give for a good conscience, which I so carelessly neglected. And what joy remains now of all my former fleshly pleasures, wherein I placed my chief delight? Those foolish pleasures were but deceitful dreams, and now they are past like vanishing shadows! But to think of those eternal pains which I must endure for those short pleasures, distresses me as hell—before I enter into hell.

Yet justly, I confess, as I have deserved I am served; that being made after God's image a reasonable soul, able to judge of my own estate, and having mercy so often offered, and I entreated to receive it—I neglected God's grace, and preferred the pleasures of sin before the pious care of pleasing God; lewdly spending my short time, without considering what accounts I must make at my last end. And now all the pleasures of my life being put together, countervail not the least part of my present pains! My joys were but momentary, and gone before I could scarcely enjoy them; my miseries are eternal, and never shall know an end. O that I had spent the hours that I consumed in card-playing, dice-throwing, and other vile exercises—in reading the scriptures, in hearing sermons, in weeping for my sins, in fasting, watching, praying, and in preparing my soul—that I might have now departed in the assured hope of everlasting salvation! O that I were now to begin my life again! How would I despise the world and its vanities! How piously and purely would I lead my life! How would I frequent the church, and use the means of grace!

If Satan should offer me all the treasures, pleasures, and promotions of this world, he could never entice me to forget these terrors of this last dreadful hour. But, O corrupt carcass and loathsome carrion! How has the devil deluded us! And how have we served and deceived each other—and pulled swift damnation upon us both! Now is my case more miserable than the beast that perishes in a ditch—for I must go to answer before the judgment-seat of the righteous Judge of heaven and earth, where I shall have none to speak for me! And these wicked fiends, who are privy to all my evil deeds, will accuse me, and I cannot excuse myself; my own heart already condemns me; I must needs therefore be damned before his judgment-seat, and from thence be carried by these infernal fiends into that horrible prison of endless torments and utter darkness, where I shall never more see light, that first most excellent thing that God made.

I, who gloried heretofore in being a free man, am now enclosed in the very claws of Satan, as the trembling partridge is within the gripping talons of the ravenous falcon. Where shall I lodge tonight—and who shall be my companions? O horror to think! O grief to consider! O cursed be the day wherein I was born—let not the day wherein my mother bore me be blessed! Cursed be the man who showed my father, saying, "A child is born unto you," and comforted him; cursed be that man because he slew me not! O that my mother's womb might have been my grave! How is it that I came forth of the womb to endure these hellish sorrows—and that my days should thus end with eternal shame? Cursed be the day that I was first united to so vile a body! O that I had but so much favor as that I might never see you more! Our parting is bitter and doleful—but our meeting again, to receive at that dreadful day the fullness of our deserved vengeance, will be far more terrible and intolerable.

But what do I mean thus—by too late lamentation, to seek to prolong time? My last hour has come, I hear the heart-strings break! This filthy house of clay falls on my head! Here is neither hope, help, nor place of any longer abiding. And must I needs be gone, you filthy carcass? O filthy carcass! Farewell, I must leave you!

But God said to him, "You fool! This very night your soul will be demanded from you. Now who will get the things you've accumulated?" (Luke 12:20). And so all trembling, the lost soul comes forth from the body, and instantly is seized upon by infernal fiends, who carry her with violence to the bottomless lake that burns with fire and brimstone; where she is kept as a prisoner in torments until the general judgment of the great day (Rev. 21:8; Jude, verse 6; 1

Pet. 3:19)

The loathsome carcass is afterwards laid in the grave. In which action, for the most part, the dead bury the dead; that is, they who are dead **in** sin, bury those who are dead **for** sin. And thus the godless and unregenerated worldling, who made earth his paradise, his belly his God, his lust his law; as in his life he sowed vanity, so he is now dead, and reaps misery. In his prosperity he neglected to serve God—in his adversity God refuses to save him! And the devil, whom he long served, now at length pays him his wages. Detestable was his life, damnable is his death. The devil has his soul, the grave has his carcass—in which pit of corruption, den of death, and dungeon of sorrow—let us leave the miserable sinner, rotting with his mouth full of earth, his belly full of worms, and his carcass full of stench; expecting a fearful resurrection, when the body shall be reunited with the soul; that as they sinned together, so they may be eternally tormented together!

Thus far of the miseries of the soul and body is death, which is but cursedness in part—Now follows the fullness of cursedness, which is the misery of the soul and body after death.

III. The misery of a man AFTER death, which is the fullness of cursedness.

The fullness of cursedness, when it falls upon a creature, not able to bear the brunt of it, presses him down to that bottomless deep of the endless wrath of Almighty God, which is called the damnation of hell (Lk. 8:28, & 16:23; 1 Th. 1:10; Mt. 23:33). This fullness of cursedness is either particular or general.

PARTICULAR is that which, in a less measure of fullness, lights upon the soul immediately, as soon as she is separated from the body (Lk. 16:22, 23; 1 Pet. 3:19; Jude, verses 6,7); for in the very instant of dissolution she is in the sight and presence of God—for when she ceases to see with the organ of fleshly eyes, she sees after a spiritual manner; like Stephen, who saw the glory of God, and Jesus standing at his right hand (Acts 7:5); or as a man who, being born blind, and miraculously restored to his sight, should see the sun, which he never saw before. And there, by the testimony of her own conscience, Christ, the righteous Judge, who knows all things, takes her, by his omnipresent power, to understand the doom and judgment that is due unto her sins, and what must be her eternal state. And in this manner standing in the sight of heaven, not fit, for her uncleanness, to come into heaven, she is said to stand before the throne of God. And so immediately she is carried by the evil demons, who come to fetch her with violence into hell, where she is kept, as in a prison, in everlasting pains and chains, under darkness, unto the judgment of the great day; but not in that extremity of torments which she shall finally receive at the last day.

The **GENERAL** fullness of cursedness is in a greater measure of fullness which shall be inflicted upon both soul and body, when, by the mighty power of Christ, the supreme Judge of heaven and earth, the soul shall be brought out of hell, and the body out of the grave, as prisoners, to receive their dreadful doom, according to their evil deeds (2 Pet. 2:9; Jude, verse 7; Rev. 11:18; Jn. 5:28, 29; Rev. 20:13). How shall the reprobate, by the roaring of the sea, the quaking of the earth, the trembling of the powers of heaven (Mt. 24:29; Lk. 21:24, 25), and terrors of heavenly signs—be driven, at the world's end, to their wits' end! Oh, what a woeful salutation will there be between the damned soul and body, at their reuniting at that terrible day!

O sink of sin, O lump of filthiness (will the **soul** say to her body), how am I compelled to re-enter you, not as to an habitation to rest—but as a prison, to be tormented! How do you appear in my sight, like Jephtha's daughter, to my great torment! Would God you had perpetually rotted in the grave, that I might never have seen you again! How shall we be confounded together to hear, before God, angels, and men—laid open all those secret sins which we committed together! Have I lost heaven for the love of such a foul carrion? Are you the flesh for whose pleasures I have yielded to commit so many fornications? O filthy belly! How did I become such a fool as to make you my god! How insane was I, for momentary joys—to incur these torments of eternal pains! You rocks and mountains—why do you skip away from me—and will not fall upon me, to hide me from the face of him who comes to sit on yonder throne; for the great day of his wrath is come, and who shall be able to stand? (Rev. 6:16, 17) Why tremble you thus, O earth, at the presence of the Lord—and will not open your mouth, and swallow me up, as you did Korah—that I may be seen no more?

O evil fiends! I would you might without delay tear me in pieces—on condition that you would tear me into nothingness!

But while you are thus in vain bewailing your misery, the angels (Mt. 13:41) drag you violently out of your grave to some place near the tribunal-seat of Christ; where being, as a cursed goat, separated to stand on the left hand of the Judge—Christ will pass sentence upon you (Mt. 25:33)

Within you, your own conscience (more than a thousand witnesses) shall accuse you. The devils, who tempted you to all your lewdness, shall on the **one side** testify with your conscience against you! And on the **other side** shall stand the holy saints and angels approving Christ's justice! **Behind** you, an hideous noise of innumerable fellow-reprobates waiting to receive you into their company! **Before** you, all the world burning in flaming fire! **Above** you, an wrathful Judge of deserved vengeance, ready to pronounce his sentence upon you! **Beneath** you, the fiery and sulphurous mouth of the bottomless pit, gaping to receive you! In this woeful estate, to hide yourself will be impossible, for you would wish that the greatest rock might fall upon you! (Rev. 6:16,17). To appear before the holy Lamb will be intolerable, and yet you must stand forth, to receive with other reprobates, this sentence—"Depart from me, you cursed one, into everlasting fire, prepared for the devil and his angels!"

Depart from Me—there is a separation from all joy and happiness.

You cursed one—there is a black and direful exclusion from a holy God.

Into fire—there is the cruelty of pain.

Everlasting—there is the perpetuity of punishment.

Prepared for the devil and his demons—there are your infernal tormenting and tormented companions.

O terrible sentence! From which the condemned cannot escape; which being pronounced, cannot possibly be withstood; against which a man cannot deny, and from which a man can nowhere appeal—so that to the damned, nothing remains but hellish torments, which know neither ease of pain, nor end of time! From this judgment-seat you must be thrust by angels, together with all the devils and reprobates, into the bottomless lake of utter darkness, that perpetually burns with fire and brimstone (Rev. 21:8). Whereunto, as you shall be thrust, there shall be such weeping, woes, and wailing, that the cry of the company of Korah, Dathan, and Abiram, when the earth swallowed them up, was nothing comparable to this howling! Nay, it will seem unto you a hell, before you go into hell—but to *hear* of it.

Into which lake, after that you are once plunged, you shall ever be falling down, and never meet a bottom; and in it you shall ever lament, and none shall pity you; you shall always weep for pain of the fire, and yet gnash your teeth for the extremity of cold; you shall weep to think, that your miseries are past remedy; you shall weep to think, that to repent is to no purpose; you shall weep

to think, how, for the 'shadows of short pleasures'—you have in-
curred these sorrows of eternal pains; you shall weep, to see how
weeping itself can nothing prevail; yes, in weeping, you shall weep
more tears than there is water in the sea; for the water of the sea
is finite—but the weeping of a reprobate shall be infinite!

There your lascivious **eyes** will be afflicted with sights of ghastly
spirits; your curious **ears** affrighted with hideous noise of devils,
and the weeping and gnashing of teeth of reprobates; your dainty
nose will be cloyed with noisome stench of sulphur; your delicate
taste pained with intolerable hunger; your drunken **throat** will be
parched with unquenchable thirst; your mind will be tormented
to think how, for the love of pleasures, which perished before they
budded—you so foolishly did lose heaven's joys, and incur hellish
pains, which last beyond eternity! Your conscience shall ever sting
you like an adder, when you think how often Christ by his preachers offered the remission of sins, and the kingdom of heaven freely
to you, if you would but believe and repent; and how easily you
might have obtained mercy in those days; how near you were many
times to have repented, and yet did allow the devil and the world
to keep you still in impenitency; and how the day of mercy is now
past, and will never dawn again. How shall your understanding be
racked, to consider, that, for momentary riches—you have lost the
eternal treasure, and exchanged heaven's felicity for hell's misery;
where every part of your body, without intermission of pain, shall
be continually tormented!

In these hellish torments you shall be forever deprived of the
beatifical sight of God, wherein consists the sovereign good and
life of the soul; you shall never see light, nor the least light of joy—
but lie in a perpetual prison of utter darkness, where there shall
be no **order**—but horror; where there shall be no **voice**—but of
blasphemers and howlers; where there shall be no **noise**—but of
tortures and tortured; where there shall be no **society**—but of the
devil and his angels, who being tormented themselves, shall have
no other ease but to wreak their fury in tormenting you; where
shall be punishment without pity; misery without mercy; sorrow
without support; crying without comfort; mischief without measure; torment without ease—where the worm dies not and the fire
is never quenched; where the wrath of God shall seize upon the
soul and body, as the flame of fire does on the brimstone. In which
flame you shall ever be **burning**, and never consumed; ever **dying**,
and never dead; ever **roaring** in the pangs of death, and never rid
of those pangs, nor knowing end of your pains.

So that after you have endured them so many *thousand years* as there are grass on the earth, or sand on the sea shore—you are no nearer to have an end of your torments, than you were the first day that you were cast into them! Yes, so far are they from ending, that they are ever but beginning! But if, after a thousand times so many thousand years, your lost soul could but conceive a hope that her torments should have an end, this would be some comfort—to think that at length an end will come. But as oft as the mind thinks of this word NEVER—it is as another hell in the midst of hell!

This thought shall force the damned to cry, "Woe! Woe!" as much as if they should say, not ever, not ever, O Lord, not ever, not ever torment us thus! But their conscience shall answer them as an echo, "Forever! Forever!" Hence shall arise their doleful woe, and alas forevermore!

This is that second death, the general complete fullness of all cursedness and misery, which every damned reprobate must suffer—so long as God and his saints shall enjoy bliss and felicity in heaven forevermore.

Thus far of the misery of man in his state of corruption—unless he is renewed by grace in Christ.

MEDITATIONS ON THE BLESSED STATE OF THOSE RECONCILED TO GOD IN CHRIST

Now let us see how happy a godly man is in his state of renovation, being reconciled to God in Christ.

The godly man whose corrupt nature is renewed by grace in Christ and become a new creature, is blessed in a threefold respect—First, in his **life**; Secondly, in his **death**; Thirdly, **after death**.

I. Meditations on the blessed state of a Christian during his LIFE

This is but in part, and that consists in seven things—

1. Because he is born of the Spirit (Jn. 3:5)—not of blood, nor of the will of the flesh, nor of the will of man—but of God (Jn. 1:13), who in Christ is his Father (Gal. 4:6, 7; 2 Cor. 9:8)—so that the image of God his Father is renewed in him every day more and more (Eph. 4:2, 3, 13; Col. 3:10)

2. He has, for the merits of Christ's sufferings—all his sins, original and actual, with the guilt and punishment belonging to them (Rom. 4:8,25; 8:1,2; 1 Pet. 2:24), freely and fully forgiven him; and all the righteousness of Christ as freely and fully imputed to him (Rom. 4:5,19); and so God is reconciled to him (2 Cor. 5:19); and approves him as righteous in his sight, on the merits of Christ (Rom. 8:33,34).

3. He is freed from Satan's bondage (Act. 16:18; Eph. 2:2), and is made a brother of Christ (Jn. 20:17; Rom. 8:20), a fellow-heir of his heavenly kingdom (Rom. 8:17), and a spiritual king and priest (Rev. 1:6), to offer up spiritual sacrifices to God by Jesus Christ (1 Pet. 2:5; Mal. 3:17)

4. God spares him as a man spares his own son that serves him. And this sparing consists in,

(1) Not taking notice of every fault—but bearing with his infirmities (Ex. 34:6, 7). A loving father will not cast his child away, just because he is sick.

(2) Not making his punishment, when he is chastened, as great as his deserts (Ps. 103:10)

(3) Chastening him moderately when he sees that he will not by any other means be reclaimed (2 Sam. 7:14, 15; 1 Cor. 11:32).

(4) Graciously accepting his endeavors, notwithstanding the imperfection of his obedience; and so preferring the willingness of his mind before the worthiness of his work (2 Cor. 8:12)

(5) Turning the curses which he deserved to fatherly corrections. Yes, turning all things, all calamities of this life, death itself, yes, his very sins, to his good (Rom. 8:28; Ps. 89:31, 33; 119:71; Heb. 12:10; 2 Cor. 12:7; 1 Cor. 15:54, 55; Heb. 2:14, 15; Lk. 22:31, 32; Ps. 51:13, 14; Rom. 5:20, 21)

5. God gives him his Holy Spirit, who,

(1) Sanctifies him by degrees throughout (1 Th. 5:23), so that he more and more dies to sin and lives to righteousness (Rom. 8:5, 10)

(2) Assures him of his adoption, and that he is by grace the child of God (Rom. 8:16)

(3) Encourages him to come with boldness and confidence into the presence of God (Heb. 4:16; Eph. 3:12).

(4) Moves him without fear to say unto him, 'Abba, Father' (Gal. 4:6; Rom. 8:15, 16)

(5) Pours into his heart the gift of sanctified prayer.

(6) Persuades him that both he and his prayers are accepted and heard of God, for Christ his mediator's sake.

(7) Fills him with, 1st, Peace of conscience (Rom. 5:1; 14:17); 2nd, Joy in the Holy Spirit (Rom. 14:17)—in comparison whereof all earthly joys seem vain and vile to him.

6. He has a recovery of his sovereignty over the creatures (Ps. 8:5; Heb. 2:7, 8), which he lost by Adam's fall; and from thence free liberty (Rom. 14:14; 1 Tim. 4:2, etc.) of using all things which God has not restrained (1 Cor. 9:19, 20), so that he may use them with a good conscience (1 Cor. 3:22, 32; Heb. 1:7). For to all things in heaven and earth he has a sure title in this life (1 Cor. 3:22); and he shall have the complete and peaceable possession of them in the life to come (Mt. 25:34; 1 Pet. 1:4). Hence it is that all reprobates are but 'usurpers' of all that they possess, and have no place of their own but hell (Acts 1:25).

7. He has the assurance of God's fatherly care and protection day and night over him; which care consists in three things:

(1) In providing all things necessary for his soul and body, concerning this life (Mt. 6:32; 2 Cor. 12:14; Ps. 23; 34:9,10), and that which is to come; so that he shall be sure ever either to have enough, or patience to be content with that he has.

(2) In that God gives his holy angels, as ministers, a charge to attend upon him always for his good (Heb. 1:14; Ps. 34:7; 91:11). Yes, in times of danger to pitch their tents about him for his safety

wherever he be. Yes, God's protection shall defend him as a cloud by day, and as a pillar of fire by night (Isa. 4:5;) and his providence shall hedge him from the power of the devil (Job 1:10).

(3) In that the eyes of the Lord are upon him, and his ears continually open, to see his state (Ps. 34:15; Gen. 7:1), and to hear his pleas for help, and in his good time to deliver him out of all his troubles (Ps. 34:19).

Thus far of the blessed state of the godly and regenerate man in this life.

Now of his blessed state in death.

II. Meditations on the blessed state of a Christian in his DEATH

When God sends death as his messenger for the regenerate man, he meets him half-way to heaven, for his thoughts and affections are in heaven before him (Phil. 3:20; Col. 3:2). Death is never strange nor fearful to him—not strange, because he died daily—not fearful, because while he lived, he was dead, and his life was hidden with Christ in God (1 Cor. 1:31; Col. 3:3). To die, therefore, is to him nothing else in effect—but **to rest from his labor in this world, to go home to his Father's house**, unto the city of the living God, the heavenly Jerusalem, to an innumerable company of angels, to the general assembly and church of the first-born, to God the Judge of all, and to the spirits of just men made perfect, and to Jesus the Mediator of the new covenant (Rev. 14:13; 2 Cor. 5:6; Jn. 14:2; Heb. 12:22).

While his body is sick, his mind is sound; for God makes his bed in sickness, and strengthens him with faith and patience, upon his bed of sorrow (Ps. 41:3). And when he begins to enter into death—the way of all the world—he gives (like Jacob, Moses, and Joshua) to his children and friends, godly exhortations and counsels, to serve the true God, to worship Him truly all the days of their life (Gen. 49). His blessed soul breaths nothing but blessings, and such speeches as savor a sanctified spirit. As his outward man decays, so his inward man increases, and waxes stronger; when the **speech** of his tongue falters, the sighs of his heart speak louder unto God; when the **sight** of the eyes fails, the Holy Spirit illuminates him inwardly with abundance of spiritual light. His soul fears not—but is bold to go out of the body, and to dwell forever with her Lord (2 Cor. 5:8). He sighs out with Paul, "I desire to depart—and to be with Christ," Phil. 1:23. And with David, "As the deer pants after the water-brooks, so my soul pants after you, O God. My soul thirsts for God, for the living God—when shall I come and appear before God?" Ps. 42:2. He prays with the saints, "How long, O Lord, holy and true?" Rev. 6:10. "Come, Lord Jesus, come quickly," Rev. 22:10.

And when the appointed time of his death is come (Job 14:5), knowing that he goes to his Father and Redeemer in the peace of a good conscience (Ps. 31:5), and the assured persuasion of the forgiveness of all his sins, in the blood of the Lamb, he sings with blessed old Simeon his Nunc dimittis, "Lord, now let you your servant depart in peace," (Lk. 2:29; Ps. 37:37; Isa. 57:2), and surrenders up his soul, as it were, with his own hands, into the hands of his heavenly Father, saying with David, "Into your hands, O Father, I commend my soul, for you have redeemed me, O God of truth," Ps. 31:5. And saying with Stephen, "Lord Jesus, receive my spirit," Acts 7:59. He no sooner yields up the Spirit—but immediately the holy angels (Mt. 18:10; Acts 12:15; 27:23) who attended upon him from his birth to his death, carry and accompany his soul into heaven, as they did the soul of Lazarus into Abraham's bosom (Lk. 16:22), which is the kingdom of heaven, where only good angels and good works do accompany the soul (Mt. 8:11; Lk. 13:28; Acts 15:10,11; Eph. 1:10; Heb. 11:9,10,16; 12:22,23; Lk. 19:9; 9:31;) the one to deliver their charge (Ps. 91:11; Heb. 1:14); the other to receive their reward (Rev. 14:13; 22:12).

The **body**, in convenient time, as the sanctified temple of the Holy Spirit (1 Cor. 6:19), the members of Christ (1 Cor. 6:15), nourished by his body (Mt. 26:26), the price of the blood of the Son of God (1 Cor. 6:20; 1 Pet. 1:19), is by his fellow-brethren reverently laid to sleep in the grave as in the bed of Christ (1 Th. 4:14; Acts 7:6; 8:2), in an assured hope to awake in the resurrection of the just, at the last day, to be partaker, with the soul, of life and glory everlasting (Dan. 12:2; Jn. 5:28,29; Lk. 14:14; 1 Th. 4:16,17; Rev. 14:13). And in this respect not only the souls—but the very bodies of the faithful also are termed blessed.

Thus far of the blessedness of the soul and body of the regenerate man in death—Now let us see the blessedness of his soul and body after death.

III. Meditations on the blessed state of a Christian AFTER DEATH.

This state has three degrees—

1. From the day of death—to the resurrection.
2. From the resurrection—to the pronouncing of the sentence.
3. After the sentence—which lasts eternally.

1. From the day of death—to the resurrection.

As soon as ever the regenerate man has yielded up his **soul** to Christ, the holy angels take her into their custody, and immediately carry her into heaven (Luke 16:22), and there present her before Christ—where she is crowned with a crown of righteousness and glory; not which she has deserved by her good works—but which God has promised of his free goodness to all those who, of love, have in this life sincerely served him, and sought his glory (Heb. 1:14; 12:24; 2 Tim. 4:8; Rev. 2:10; 1 Pet. 5:4)

Oh, what joy will it be to your soul, which was accustomed to see nothing but misery and sinners on earth—now to behold the face of the God of glory! Yes, to see Christ welcoming you, as soon as you are presented before him by the holy angels, with a "Well done! Welcome good and faithful servant! Enter into your Master's joy!" And what joy will this be, to behold thousand thousands of cherubim, seraphim, angels, thrones, dominions, principalities, powers! (Col. 1:6; Eph. 1:21) All the holy patriarchs, priests, prophets, apostles, martyrs, confessors, and all the souls of your Christian friends, parents, husbands, wives, children, and the rest of God's saints, who departed before you in the true faith of Christ—standing before God's throne in bliss and glory!

If the Queen of Sheba, beholding the glory and majesty of Solomon, was ravished therewith, and broke out and said, "Happy are your men, happy are these your servants, which stand ever before you, and hear your wisdom," (1 Ki. 10:8), how shall your soul he ravished to see herself, by grace, admitted to stand with this glorious company, to behold the blessed face of Christ, and to hear all the treasures of his divine wisdom! How shall you rejoice to see so many thousand thousands welcoming you into their heavenly society (Lk. 15); for as they all rejoiced at your *conversion*—so will they now be much more joyful to behold your *coronation*—and to see you receive your crown, which was reserved for your coming (1 Tim. 4:8).

There the crown of **martyrdom** shall be put on the head of the martyr, who for Christ's gospel's sake endured torments. The crown of **piety** shall be put on the head of the head of them who sincerely professed Christ. The crown of **good works** shall be put on the head of the good alms-giver's head, who liberally relieved the poor. The crown of **incorruptible glory** shall be put on the head of the head of those who by their preaching and good example have converted souls from the corruption of sin, to glorify God in holiness of life. Who can sufficiently express the rejoicing of this heavenly company, to see you thus crowned with glory (Rev. 7:9), arrayed with the shining robes of righteousness, and to behold the palm of victory put into your hand!

O what thanks and praise will you have, that, by God's grace, you have escaped all the miseries of the world, all the snares of the devil, all the pains of hell—and received eternal rest and happiness! For there everyone rejoices as much in another's happiness as in his own, because he shall see him as much loved of God as himself; yes, they have as many distinct joys as they have copartners of their joy. And in this joyful and blessed state, the soul rests with Christ in heaven until the resurrection; when the number of her fellow-servants and brethren shall have been fulfilled, which the Lord terms 'but a little season' (Rev. 7:9)

II. The second degree of man's blessedness after death, is **from the resurrection—to the pronouncing of the final sentence**. For at the last day:

1. The elementary heavens, earth, and all things therein, shall be dissolved, and purified with fire (2 Pet. 2:10,12,13)

2. At the sound of the last trumpet, or voice of Christ, the Archangel—the very same bodies which the elect had before (though turned to dust and earth) shall arise again (1 Cor. 15:52; 1 Th. 4:16; Jn. 5:28; Ezek. 37:7, 8, etc). And in the same instant, every man's soul shall re-enter into his own body, by virtue of the resurrection of Christ, their head (Rom. 8:11; Phil. 3:10,11; 1 Th. 4:14), and be made alive and rise out of their graves, as if they did but awake out of their beds of sleep (Rom. 5:17; 1 Cor. 15:22). And howsoever tyrants bemangled their bodies in pieces, or consumed them to ashes—yet shall the elect find it true at that day, that not a hair of their head has perished (Mt. 19:30)

3. They shall come forth out of their graves, like so many Josephs out of prison; or Daniels out of the lion's den; or Jonahs out of the whale's belly; (1 Th. 4:14; Dan. 6:23).

4. All the **bodies** of the elect being thus made alive, shall arise in that perfection of nature whereunto they would have attained by their natural temperament, if no impediment had hindered (Isa. 65:20); and in that vigor of age that a perfect man is—at about thirty-three years old, each in their proper gender. To which divines think the apostle alludes when he says, "Until we all come unto a perfect man, unto the measure of the age (or stature) of the fullness of Christ," Eph. 4:13. Whatever imperfection was before in the body (as blindness, lameness, crookedness) shall then be done away. Jacob shall not halt, nor Isaac be blind, nor Leah weak-eyed, nor Mephibosheth lame. For if David would not have the blind and lame to come into his house, much less will Christ have blindness and lameness to dwell in his heavenly habitation. Christ made all the blind to see, the mute to speak, the deaf to hear, the lame to walk—who came to him to seek his grace on earth—much more will he heal all their imperfections whom he will admit to his glory in heaven! Among those tribes, there is not one feeble; but the lame man shall leap as a deer, and the mute man's tongue shall sing (Ps. 105:37; Isa. 35:6). And it is very probable, that seeing God created our first parents, not infants, or old men—but of a perfect age or stature—the new creation from death, shall every way be more perfect than the first frame of man, from which he fell into the state of the dead. Neither is it like that time of infancy—being imperfection; or of old age—being corruption—which are not consistent with the state of a perfect glorified body.

5. The bodies of the elect being thus raised, shall have four most excellent and supernatural qualities. "So it is with the resurrection of the dead: Sown in corruption, raised in **incorruption**; sown in dishonor, raised in **glory**; sown in weakness, raised in **power**; sown a natural body, raised a spiritual body." (1 Corinthians 15:42-44)

(1) They shall be raised in **power**, whereby they shall forever be freed from all wants and weakness, and enabled to continue, without the use of food, drink, sleep, and other former helps (1 Cor. 15:43).

(2) In **incorruption**, whereby they shall never be subject to any manner of imperfections, blemish, sickness, or death (1 Cor. 15:41; Isa. 65:20)

(3) In **glory**, whereby their bodies shall shine as bright as the sun in the skies (Mt. 13:43; Lk. 9:31) and which being made transparent, their souls shall shine through far more glorious than their bodies (1 Th. 4:17).

There are three glimpses of which glory were seen—first, in Moses' face (Ex. 34:29); secondly, in the Transfiguration (Mt. 17:2); thirdly, in Stephen's countenance (Acts 6:15). These are three instances and assurances of the glorification of our bodies at that glorious day. Then shall the mourner lay aside his mourning garments, and put on the robe of the King's Son, Jesus. Then every true Mordecai (who mourned under the sackcloth of this corrupt flesh) shall be arrayed with the King's royal apparel (Est. 6:4), and have the royal crown set upon his head, that all the world may see what shall be done to him whom the King of kings delights to honor. If now the rising of one sun makes the morning so glorious, how glorious shall that day be, when innumerable millions of millions of bodies of saints and angels shall appear more glorious than the brightness of the sun—the body of Christ in glory surpassing all!

(4) In **agility**, whereby our bodies shall be able to ascend, and meet the Lord at his glorious coming in the air, as eagles flying unto their blessed homes. To this agility of the glorious bodies of the saints the prophet alludes, saying, "They shall renew their strength; they shall mount up with wings as eagles; they shall run, and not be weary; they shall walk, and not faint," Isa. 40:31. And to this state may that saying of Wisdom be referred—"In the time of their vision they shall shine, and run to and fro, as sparks among the stubble."

And in respect of these four qualities, Paul calls the raised bodies of the elect **spiritual** (1 Cor. 15:46)—for they shall be spiritual in qualities—but the same still in substance.

And howsoever sin and corruption make a man, in this state of mortality, lower than angels, yet surely, when God shall thus crown him with glory and honor (Ps. 8:5), man shall be superior to angels. For are they spirits? So is man also in respect of his soul—yes, more than this, they shall have also a spiritual body, fashioned like unto the glorious body of the Lord Jesus Christ (Phil. 3:21)—an honor which he never gave to angels—and in this respect man has a prerogative above them. Nay, they are but spirits appointed to be ministers unto the elect (Heb. 1:14; Ps. 91:11); and as many of them, who at the first disdained this office, and would not keep their first estate, were for their pride hurled into hell (Jude, verse 6; 2 Pet. 2:4). This lessens not the dignity of angels—but extols the greatness of God's love to his redeemed people.

But as for all the elect, who at that second and sudden coming of Christ shall be found still living—when the fire that shall burn up the corruption of the world, and the works therein—shall in a moment, in the twinkling of an eye, burn up the dross and corruption of their mortality, and make them immortal bodies. This change shall be unto them, instead of death.

Then shall the **soul** with joyfulness greet her **body**, saying—O we meet again, my dear sister! How sweet is your voice! How lovely is your countenance—even after having lain hidden so long in the clefts of the rocks, and in the secret places of the grave! (Song 2:14). You are indeed a habitation fit, not only for me to dwell in—but such as the Holy Spirit thinks fit to reside in—as his temple, forever. The winter of our affliction is now past; the storm of our misery is blown over and gone. The bodies of our elect brethren appear more glorious than the lily-flowers on the earth; the time of singing hallelujah is come, and the voice of the trumpet is heard in the land. You have been my associate in the Lord's labors, and companion in persecutions and wrongs, for Christ and his gospel's sake. Now shall we enter together into our Master's joy. As you have borne with me the cross—so shall you now wear with me the crown. As you have with me sowed plenteously in tears—so shall you reap with me abundantly in joy. O blessed, ever blessed be that God, who, when yonder reprobates spent their whole time in pride, fleshly lusts, eating, drinking, and profane vanities—gave us grace to join together in watching, fasting, praying, reading the scriptures, keeping his commandments, hearing sermons, receiving the holy communion, relieving the poor, exercising, in all humility, the works of piety to God, and walking uprightly in all our duties towards men. You shall, henceforth, hear no mention of your sins—for they are forgiven and covered (Ps. 32:1). But every good work which you have done for the Lord's sake—shall be rehearsed and rewarded.

Cheer up your heart, for your Judge is flesh of your flesh, and bone of your bone (Dan. 9:21). Lift up your head, behold these glorious angels, like so many Gabriels, flying towards us, to tell us that the day of our redemption has come (Lk. 21:28), and to convey us in the clouds to meet our Redeemer in the air. behold, they are at hand! Arise, therefore, my dove, my love, my lovely one— and come away (Song 2:1,3). And so, like young deer (verse 17), they run with angels towards Christ, over the trembling 'mountains of division'.

6. Both living and dead being thus revived and glorified, shall instantly, by the ministry of God's holy angels (Lk. 17:34, 35, 36), be gathered from all the quarters and parts of the world, and caught up together in the clouds, to meet the Lord in the air (1 Th. 4:17), and so shall come with him, as a part of his glorious retinue—to judge the reprobates and evil angels (1 Cor. 6:1, 3). The twelve apostles shall sit upon twelve thrones (next Christ) to judge the twelve tribes, who refused to hear the gospel preached by their ministry. And all the saints, in honor and order, shall stand next to them, as judges also, to judge the evil angels, and earthly-minded men (1 Cor. 6:2, 3). And as some of them received grace in this life to be more zealous for his glory, and more faithful in his service, than others—so shall their glory and reward be greater than others in that day (Rev. 22:12; 2 Cor. 5:6)

The **place** where they shall be gathered unto Christ, and where Christ shall sit in judgment, shall be in the **air** (1 Th. 4:17), over the valley of Jehoshaphat, by Mount Olivet, near to Jerusalem, eastward from the temple, as it is probable, for four reasons—

1. Because the holy scripture seems to intimate so much in plain words—"I will gather all nations into the valley of Jehoshaphat and plead with them there. Cause your mighty one to come down, O Lord—let the heathen be awakened and come up to the valley of Jehoshaphat; for there will I sit to judge all the heathen round about," Joel 3:1,2,11,12. Jehoshaphat signifies, 'the Lord will judge'. And this valley was so called from the great victory which the Lord gave Jehoshaphat and his people over the Ammonites, Moabites, and inhabitants of Mount Seir (2 Chr. 20); which victory was a type of the final victory which Christ, the Supreme Judge, shall give his elect over all their enemies in that place at the last day, as also the Jews interpret it—(see Zech. 14:4,5; Ps. 51:1,2)—all agreeing that the place shall be thereabouts.

2. Because that as Christ was thereabouts crucified and put to open shame, so over that place his glorious throne should be erected in the air, when he shall appear in judgment to manifest his majesty and glory. For it is fit that Christ should in that place judge the world with righteous judgment—where he himself was unjustly judged and condemned.

3. Because that seeing the angels shall be sent to gather together the elect from the four winds, from one end of heaven to the other, it is most probable that the place where they shall be gathered to shall be near Jerusalem and the valley of Jehoshaphat; which geographers describe to be in the midst of the surface of the earth.

4. Because the angels told the disciples that as they saw Christ ascend from Mount Olivet (Acts 1:11), which is over the valley of Jehoshaphat, so he shall in like manner come down from heaven.

5. Lastly, When Christ is set in his glorious throne, and all the many thousands of his saints and angels, shining more bright than so many suns in glory, sitting around him (Mt. 25:31; Jude, verse 14; Rev. 20:11,12), and the body of Christ in glory and brightness surpassing them all; the reprobates being separate, and remaining beneath upon the earth (for the right hand signifies a blessed, the left hand a cursed estate), Christ will first pronounce the sentence of bliss upon the elect (Mt. 19:28) and he will thereby increase the grief of the reprobate who shall hear it, and he will show himself more prone to mercy than to judgment (Ps. 145:9; Isa. 28:21). And thus, from his throne of majesty in the air, he will, in the sight and

hearing of all the world, pronounce unto his elect, "Come you who are blessed by my Father—inherit the kingdom prepared for you, from the beginning of the world! For I was hungry, etc." Mt. 25:34.

Come you. Here is our blessed union with Christ, and, by him, with the whole Trinity.

Blessed. Here is our absolution from all sins, and our complete endowment with all grace and happiness.

By my Father. Here is the author from whom proceeds our felicity.

Inherit. Here is our adoption.

The kingdom. Behold our birth-right and possession.

Prepared. See God's fatherly care for his chosen ones.

From the foundation of the world. O the free, eternal, unchangeable election of God!

How much are those souls bound to love God, who of his mere good will and pleasure chose and loved them before they had done either good or evil (Rom. 9:3).

For I was hungry, etc. O the goodness of Christ, who takes notice of all the good works of his children to reward them! How great is his love to poor Christians, who takes every work of mercy done to them for his sake, as if it had been done to himself!

Come you to Me, in whom you have believed before you saw me (Jn. 20:29; 1 Pet. 1:8), and whom you have loved and sought for, with so much devotion, and through so many tribulations. Come now from labor to rest; from disgrace to glory; from the jaws of death to the joys of eternal life! For my sake you have been railed upon, reviled, and cursed (Mt. 5:11); but now it shall appear to all those cursed Esaus, that you are the true Jacobs that shall receive your heavenly Father's blessing; and blessed shall you be. Your fathers, mothers, and nearest kindred, forsook and cast you off for my truth's sake which you maintained (Ps. 27:10; Mt. 19:29); but now my Father will be unto you a father, and you shall be his sons and daughters forever (Jn. 20:17; 2 Cor. 6:18). You were cast out of your lands and livings, and forsook all for my sake and the gospel's—but that it may appear that you have not lost your gain—but gained by your loss, instead of an earthly inheritance and possessions, you shall possess with me the inheritance of my heavenly kingdom; where you shall be for love—sons; for birth-right—heirs; for dignity—kings; for holiness—priests; and you may be bold to enter into the possession of it now, because my Father prepared and kept it for you ever since the first foundation of the world was laid!

Immediately after this sentence of absolution of sin and benediction of blessings, every believer receives his crown, which Christ the righteous Judge puts upon their heads, as the reward which he has promised, of his grace and mercy—to the faith and good works of all those who loved his appearing (2 Tim. 4:8; 1 Pet. 5:4). Then everyone taking his crown from his head, shall lay it down, as it were, at the feet of Christ; and prostrating themselves, shall with one heart and voice, in a heavenly manner and harmony, say, "Praise, and honor, and glory, and power, and thanks, be unto you, O blessed Lamb, who sits upon the throne! You were killed, and have redeemed us to God by your blood—out of every kindred, and tongue, and people, and nation—and have made us unto kings and priests our God, to reign with you in your kingdom for evermore. Amen." (Rev. 4:10)

Then shall they sit upon their thrones as judges of the reprobates, and evil angels (1 Cor. 6:1, 2, 3, etc.; Mt. 19:13), by approving, and giving testimony to the righteous sentence and judgment of Christ the Supreme Judge.

After the pronouncing of the reprobates' sentence and condemnation, Christ will perform two solemn actions—

1. The presenting of all the elect unto his Father. "Behold, O righteous Father, these are they whom you have given me—I have kept them, and none of them is lost. I gave them your word, and they believed it, and the world hated them, because they were not of the world, even as I was not of the world. And now, Father, I desire that those whom you have given me, be with me where I am—that they may behold my glory, which you have given me; and that I may be in them, and you in me, that they may be made perfect in unity—that the world may know that you have sent me, and that you have loved them—as you have loved me." (Jn. 17:12, 14, 23, 24)

2. Christ shall deliver up the kingdom to God, even the Father. That is, he shall cease to execute his office of mediatorship (1 Cor. 25:24); whereby, as he is King, Priest, Prophet, and Supreme Head of the Church, he suppressed his enemies, and ruled his faithful people by his spirit, word, and sacraments—so that his kingdom of grace over his church in this world ceasing—he shall rule directly in his kingdom of glory evermore. Not that the dignity of his manhood shall be anything diminished; but that the glory of his Godhead shall be more manifested—so that as he is God, he shall from thenceforth in all fullness, without all external means—rule all in all.

From this tribunal-seat, Christ shall arise, and with all his glo-

rious company of elect angels and saints, he shall go up trium-
phantly, in order and array, unto the heaven of heavens, with
such a heavenly noise and music, that now may that song of David be truly verified, "God is gone up with a triumph, the Lord
with the sound of the trumpets. Sing praises to God, sing praises,
sing praises to our King, sing praises—for God is the King of all
the earth, he is greatly to be exalted." (Ps. 47:4,5,6,8) And that
marriage-song of John, "Let us be glad and rejoice, and give hon-
or to him; for the marriage of the Lamb has come, and his wife
has made herself ready. Hallelujah; for the Lord God Omnipotent
reigns." (Rev. 19:6,7)

The third and last degree of the blessed state of a regenerate
man after death, begins after the pronouncing of the sentence,
and lasts eternally without all end.

III. Meditations of the blessed state of a Regenerate Man in HEAVEN.

Here my meditation dazzles, and my pen falls out of my hand;
the one being not able to conceive, nor the other to describe, that
most excellent bliss, and eternal weight of glory (2 Cor. 4:17; Rom.
8:18)—whereof all the afflictions of this present life are not worthy
to be compared—which all the elect shall with the blessed Trinity
enjoy, from that time that they shall be received with Christ, as
joint-heirs (Rom. 8:17) into that everlasting kingdom of joy.

Notwithstanding, we may take a glimpse thereof. The holy scriptures thus set forth (to our capacity) the glory of our eternal and
heavenly life after death, in four respects—

1. Of the place of heaven.
2. Of the object of heaven.
3. Of the privileges of the elect in heaven.
4. Of the effects of these privileges.

1. The PLACE of heaven.

The place is the heaven of heavens, or the third heaven, called
paradise (Ps. 19:5; 2 Cor. 12:24); where Christ (in his human nature) ascended far above all visible heavens. The bridegroom's
chamber (Ps. 19:6; Mt. 25:10), which by the skies, as by an azured
curtain spangled with glittering stars, and glorious planets, is hidden, that we cannot behold it with these corruptible eyes of flesh.
The Holy Spirit condescending to our weakness, describes the glory of that place (which no man can estimate) by such things as are
most precious in the estimation of man; and therefore likens it to a
great and holy city, named the heavenly Jerusalem (Rev. 21), where
only God and his people who are saved, and written in the Lamb's

book (verses 24 & 27), do inhabit. This heavenly city is all built of pure gold, like unto clear glass or crystal (verses 11,18,19,20); the walls of jasper-stone—the foundations of the walls garnished with twelve kinds of precious stones, having twelve gates, each built of one pearl (verse 21)—three gates towards each of the four corners of the world (verse 13), and at each gate an angel (verse 12), as so many guards, that no unclean thing should enter into it (verse 27). The city is laid out in a square (verse 16), therefore perfect—the length, the breadth, and height of it are equal, 12,000 furlongs every way; therefore glorious and spacious. Through the midst of her streets ever runs a pure river of the water of life, as clear as crystal (Rev. 22:1); and on the other side the river is the tree of life (verse 2), ever growing, which bears twelve kinds of fruits, and gives fruit every month; and the leaves of the tree are health to the nations.

There is therefore no place so glorious by creation, so beautiful with delectation, so rich in possession, so comfortable for habitation. For there, the king is Christ—the law is love—the honor is verity—the peace is felicity—the life is eternity. There is light without darkness, mirth without sadness, health without sickness, wealth without want, credit without disgrace, beauty without blemish, ease without labor, riches without rust, blessedness without misery, and consolation that never knows an end. How truly may we cry out with David, of this city, "Glorious things are spoken of you, O you city of God!" Ps. 87:3. And yet all these things are spoken but according to the weakness of our capacity. For heaven exceeds all this in glory, so far, as that no tongue is able to express, nor heart of man to conceive, the glory thereof, as witnesses Paul (2 Cor. 12:4; 1 Cor. 2:5), who was in it, and saw it. O let us not then dote so much upon our present wooden cottages, and houses of moldering clay, which are but the tents of ungodliness, and habitation of sinners; but let us look rather, and long for this heavenly city, whose builder and maker is God (Heb. 11:10); which he, who is not ashamed to be called our God, has prepared for us (Heb. 11:6).

2. The OBJECT of heaven.

The blissful and glorious object of all intellectual and reasonable creatures in heaven is the Godhead, in Trinity of Persons, without which there is neither joy nor felicity; but the very fullness of joy consists in enjoying the same.

This object we shall enjoy two ways—

1. By a beatific vision of God.
2. By possessing an immediate communion with this divine nature.

The beatifical vision of God is that alone, which can content the infinite mind of man. For everything tends to its center. God is the center of the soul—therefore, like Noah's dove, she cannot rest nor joy until she return and enjoy him.

All that God bestowed upon Moses could not satisfy his mind, unless he might see the face of God (Ex. 3:13)—therefore the whole church prays so earnestly, "God be merciful unto us, and cause his face to shine upon us." (Ps. 67:1, and 80:1). When Paul once had seen this blessed sight, he ever after counted all the riches and glory of the world (in respect of it) to be but rubbish (Phil. 3:8,11); and all his life after was but a sighing out, "I desire to be dissolved, and to be with Christ." (Phil. 1:23). And Christ prayed for all his elect in his last prayer, that they might obtain this blessed vision—"Father, I will that those whom you have given me be where?—even where I am. To what end?—that they may behold my glory." (Jn. 17:14).

If Moses' face did so shine, when he had been with God but forty days, and seen but his back parts (Ex. 34:29; 33:31), how shall we shine, when we shall see him face to face forever, and know him as we are known, and as he is! (1 Cor. 13:12; 2 Cor. 3:18; 1 Jn. 3:2) Then shall the soul no longer be termed Marah, bitterness—but Naomi, beautifulness; for the Lord shall turn her short bitterness to an eternal beauty and blessedness (Ruth 1:20)

The second means to enjoy this object is, by **having an immediate and an eternal communion with God in heaven**. This we have—first, by being, as members of Christ, united to his manhood, and as by the manhood, personally united to the Word, we are united to him, as he is God; and, by his Godhead, to the whole Trinity. Reprobates at the last day see God, as a just Judge, to punish them; but, for lack of this communion, they shall have neither grace with him, nor glory from him. For lack of this communion, the devils, when they saw Christ, cried out, "What have we to do with you, O Son of the most high God?" (Mk. 5:7) But, by virtue of this communion, the penitent soul may boldly go and say unto Christ, as Ruth unto Boaz (Ruth 3:9), "Spread, O Christ, the wing of the garment of your mercy over your handmaid; for you are my kinsman." This communion God promised Abraham, when he gave himself for his great reward (Gen. 15:1) And Christ prays for his whole church to obtain it (Jn. 17:20,21). This communion Paul expresses in one word, saying, that God shall be all in all to us (1 Cor. 15:28). Indeed, God is now all in all to us; but by means, and in a small measure. But in heaven, God himself immediately, in fullness of measure, without all means, will be unto us all the good things that our souls and bodies can wish or desire. He himself will be salvation and joy to our souls, life and health to our bodies, beauty to our eyes, music to our ears, honey to our mouths, perfume to our nostrils, light to our understandings, contentment to our wills, and delight to our hearts.

And what can be lacking, where God himself will be the soul of our souls? Yes, all the strength, wit, pleasures, virtues, colors, beauties, harmony, and goodness, that are in men, animals, fish, fowls, trees, herbs, and all creatures—are nothing but sparkles of those things which are in infinite perfection in God. And in him we shall enjoy them in a far more perfect and blessed manner. He himself will then supply their use—nay, the best creatures which serve us now shall not have the honor to serve us then. There will be no need of the sun nor of the moon to shine in that city; for the glory of God does light it (Rev. 21:23). No more will there be any need or use of any creature, when we shall enjoy the Creator himself.

When, therefore, we behold anything that is excellent in any creatures, let us say to ourselves—How much more excellent is he who gave them this excellency! When we behold the **wisdom** of men, who overrule creatures stronger than themselves; outrun the sun and moon in discourse, prescribing many years before in what courses they shall be eclipsed; let us say to ourselves—how admirable is the wisdom of God, who made men so wise! When we consider the **strength** of whales and elephants, the tempest of winds, and terror of thunder, let us say to ourselves—how strong, how mighty, how dreadful is that God, who makes these mighty and fearful creatures! When we taste things that are delicately **sweet**, let us say to ourselves—O how sweet is that God from whom all these creatures have received their sweetness! When we behold the admirable **colors** which are in flowers and birds, and all the lovely **beauty** of nature, let us say—How beautiful is that God that made these so lovely!

And if our loving God has thus provided us so many excellent delights, for our passage through this Bochim (Jud. 2:5), or valley of tears, what are those pleasures which he has prepared for us, when we shall enter into the palace of our Master's joy! How shall our souls be there ravished with the love of so lovely a God! So glorious is the object of heavenly saints—so amiable is the sight of our gracious Savior!

3. Of the PRIVILEGES which the Elect shall enjoy in Heaven.

By reason of this communion with God, the elect in heaven shall have four superexcellent privileges:

1. They shall have the kingdom of heaven for their inheritance (Mt. 25; 1 Pet. 1:4), and they shall be free citizens of the heavenly Jerusalem (Eph. 2:19; Heb. 12:22). Paul, by being a free citizen of Rome (Acts 21:26), escaped whipping; but they who are once free citizens of the heavenly Jerusalem, shall ever be freed from the whips of eternal torments. For this freedom was bought for us, not with a great sum of money (Acts 22:28)—but with the precious blood of the Son of God (1 Pet. 1:18).

2. They shall all be kings and priests (Rev. 5:10; 1Pet. 2:9; Rom. 16:10)—spiritual kings, to reign with Christ, and to triumph over Satan and the world; and spiritual priests, to offer to God the spiritual sacrifice of praise and thanksgiving for evermore (1Pet. 2:5; Heb. 13:15). And therefore they are said to wear both crowns and robes. O what a comfort is this to poor parents that have many children! If they breed them up in the fear of God, and to be true Christians, then are they parents to so many kings and priests.

3. Their bodies shall shine as the brightness of the sun in the skies, like the glorious body of Christ (Mt. 13:43), which shined brighter than the sun at noon, when it appeared to Paul (Phil. 3:21; Acts 12:6). A glimpse of which glorious brightness appeared in the bodies of Moses and Elijah, transfigured with our Lord in the holy mount (Lk. 9:30; Mk. 9:5). Therefore, says the apostle, it shall rise a glorious body; yes, a spiritual body, not in substance— but in quality (1 Cor. 15:43,44)—preserved by spiritual means, and having (as an angel) agility to ascend or descend. O what an honor is it, that our bodies (falling more vile than carrion) should thus arise in glory, like unto the body of the Son of God! (1Th. 4:1)

4. Lastly, They (together with all the holy angels) there keep, without any labor to distract them, a perpetual Sabbath, to the glory, honor, and praise of God, for the creating, redeeming, and sanctifying the church; and for his power, wisdom, justice, mercy, and goodness, in the government of heaven and earth. When you hear a sweet concert of music, meditate how happy you shall be, when, with the choir of heavenly angels and saints, you shall sing a part in that spiritual Hallelujah, in that eternal blessed Sabbath, where there shall be such variety of pleasures, and satiety of joys—as neither know tediousness in doing, nor end in delighting.

4. The EFFECTS of those privileges which the Elect shall enjoy in Heaven.

From these privileges there will arise to the elect in heaven, five notable effects—

1. They shall know God with a perfect KNOWLEDGE (1 Cor. 1:10), so far as creatures can possibly comprehend the Creator. For there we shall see the Word, the Creator; and in the Word, all creatures that by the Word were created. The most excellent creatures in this life, are but as a dark veil (1 Cor. 23:12; 2 Cor. 3:16) drawn between God and us; but when this veil shall be drawn aside, then shall we see God face to face, and know him as we are known. We shall know the power of the Father, the wisdom of the Son, the grace of the Holy Spirit, and the indivisible nature of the blessed Trinity. And in him we shall know, not only all our friends who died in the faith of Christ—but also all the faithful that ever were, or shall be. For,

(1) Christ tells the Jews that they shall see Abraham, Isaac, and Jacob, and all the prophets, in the kingdom of God (Lk. 13:28); therefore we shall know them,

(2) Adam in his innocence knew Eve to be bone of his bone, and flesh of his flesh (Gen. 2:23), as soon as he awakened; much more then shall we know our kindred, when we shall awake perfected and glorified in the resurrection.

(3) The apostles knew Christ after his resurrection, and the saints which rose with him, and appeared in the holy city (Mt. 27:53).

(4) Peter, James, and John, knew Moses and Elijah in the transfiguration (Mt. 17:4); how much more shall we know one another, when we shall be all glorified?

(5) Dives knew Lazarus in Abraham's bosom (Lk. 16:23;) much more shall the elect know one another in heaven.

(6) Christ says that the twelve apostles shall sit upon twelve thrones (Mt. 19:28), to judge (at that day) the twelve tribes (1 Cor. 6:2,3); therefore they shall be known, and consequently the rest of the saints.

(7) Paul says, that at that day we shall know as we are known of God (1 Cor. 13:11); and Augustine out of this place comforts a widow, assuring her, that as in this life she saw her husband with external eyes, so in the life to come she should know his heart, and what were all his thoughts and imaginations. Then, husbands and wives, look to your actions and thoughts; for all shall be made manifest one day (See 1 Cor. 4:5).

(8) The faithful in the Old Testament, are said to be gathered to their fathers (Gen. 25:35; 2 Ki. 22); therefore the knowledge of our friends remains.

(9) Love never fails (1 Cor. 13:8); therefore knowledge, the ground thereof, remains in another life.

(10) Because the last day shall be a declaration of the just judgment of God, when he shall reward every man according to his works (Rom. 2:5; Rev. 22:12; Eccl. 12:14; Rom. 2:16); and if every man's work be brought to light, much more the worker. And if wicked men shall account for every idle word (Mt. 12:36), much more shall the idle speakers themselves be known. And if the people be not known, in vain are the works made manifest. "Therefore," says the apostle, "every man shall appear, to give an account for the work that he has done in his body," 1 Cor. 5:10. Though the respect of diversities of degrees and callings in magistracy, ministry, and business shall cease; yes, Christ shall then cease to rule, as he is Mediator (1 Cor. 15:14, 28), and rule all in all, as he is God equal with the Father and the Holy Spirit.

The greatest knowledge that men can attain to in this life (1 Cor. 13:11) comes as far short of the knowledge which we shall have in heaven, as the knowledge of a child that cannot yet speak plain, comes of the knowledge of the greatest philosopher in the world. They who thirst for knowledge, let them long to be students of this university. For all the light by which we know anything in this world, is nothing but the very shadow of God; but when we shall know God in heaven, we shall in him know the manner of the work of the creation, the mysteries of the work of our redemption; yes, so much knowledge as a creature can possibly conceive and comprehend of the Creator and his works. But while we are in this life, we may say with Job, "How little a portion hear we of him?" Job 26:14.

2. They shall LOVE God with as perfect and absolute a love as possibly a creature can do. The *manner* of loving God, is to love him for himself (1Cor. 13:12); the *measure* is to love him without measure. For in this life (knowing God but in part) we love him but in part; but when the elect in heaven shall fully know God, then they will perfectly love God—and for the infinite causes of love, which they shall know to be in Him, they shall be infinitely ravished with the love of Him.

3. They shall be filled with all kinds of divine PLEASURES. "At your right hand," says David, "there are pleasures for evermore," Ps. 16:11; "Yes, they shall drink," says he, "out of the river of pleasures," Ps. 36:8. For as soon as the soul is admitted into the actual fruition of the beatifical essence of God, she has all the goodness, beauty, glory, and perfection of all creatures, in all the worlds united together, and at once presented to her in the sight of God. If any delight in beauty, the fairest beauty is but a dusky shadow compared to that. He that delights in pleasures shall there find infinite varieties, without either interruption of grief, or distraction of pain. He that loves honor shall there enjoy it, without the disgrace of cankered envy. He that loves treasure shall there possess it, and never be beguiled of it. There they shall have knowledge void of all ignorance, health that no sickness shall impair, and life that no death can determine. How happy, then, shall we be, when this life is changed, and we translated there!

4. They shall be replenished with an unspeakable JOY. "In your presence," says David, "is the fullness of joy." (Ps. 16:11) And this joy shall arise chiefly from the vision of God, and partly from the sight of all the holy angels, and blessed souls of just and perfect men, who are in bliss and glory with them; but especially from the blissful sight of Jesus, the Mediator of the New Testament, our Emmanuel, God made man. The sight of Jesus will be the chief cause of our bliss and joy. If the Israelites in Jerusalem so shouted for joy, that the earth rang again, to see Solomon crowned, how shall the elect rejoice in heaven, to see Christ, the true Solomon, adorned with glory! If John the Baptist, at his presence, did leap in his mother's womb for joy, how shall we exult for joy, when he will be with us in heaven! If the wise men rejoiced so greatly to find him a babe, lying in a manger, how great shall the joy of the elect be, to see him sit, as a king, in his celestial throne! If Simeon was glad to see him an infant, in the temple, presented by the hands of the priest, how great shall our joy be to see him a king, ruling all things, at the right hand of his Father! If Joseph and Mary were so joyful to find him in the midst of the doctors in the temple, how glad shall our souls be, to see him sitting, as Lord, among angels in heaven! This is that joy of our Master, which, as the apostle says, "the eye has not seen, the ear has not heard, nor the heart of man can conceive." (1 Cor. 2:5; Mt. 25:21); which, because it cannot enter into us—we shall enter into it.

5. Lastly, They shall enjoy this blissful and glorious state FOREVER—therefore it is termed everlasting life (Jn. 17:3). And Christ says, that our joy shall no man take from us. All other joys, be they ever so great, have an end. Ahasuerus' feast lasted an hundred and eighty days (Est. 1:3)—but he, and it, and all his joys are gone. For mortal man to be assumed to heavenly glory, to be associated to angels, to be satiated with all delights and joys—but for a time, were much—but to enjoy them forever, without intermission or end, who can hear it, and not admire? All the saints of Christ, as soon as they felt once but a true taste of these eternal joys, counted all the riches and pleasures of this life to be but loss and rubbish, in comparison to that (Phil. 3:8). And therefore, with incessant prayers, fasting, alms-deeds, tears, faith, and holy living, they labored to ascertain themselves of this eternal life; and for the love of it, they willingly either sold or parted with all their earthly goods and possessions (Acts 2:45).

Christ calls Christians merchants (Lk. 14), and eternal life a precious pearl, which a wise merchant will purchase, though it cost him all that he has (Mt. 13).

Alexander hearing the report of the great riches of the eastern country, divided immediately among his captains and soldiers, all his kingdom of Macedonia. Hephæstion asking him, What he meant in so doing? Alexander answered, That he preferred the riches of India (whereof he hoped shortly to be master) before all that his father Philip had left him in Macedonia. And should not Christians, then, prefer the eternal riches of heaven, so greatly renowned (which they shall enjoy before long), before the corruptible things of this world, which last but for a season?

Abraham and Sarah left their own country and possessions, to look for a city whose builder and maker is God (Heb. 11:10,15,16); and therefore bought no land, but only a place of burial. David preferred one day with God, more than a thousand elsewhere; yes, to be a door-keeper in the house of God, rather than to dwell in the richest tabernacles of wickedness (Ps. 134:10). Elijah earnestly besought the Lord to receive his soul into his kingdom (1Ki. 19:4), and went willingly, though in a fiery chariot, there (2Ki. 2:11). Paul, having once seen heaven, continually desired to be dissolved, that he might be with Christ (Phil. 1:23). Peter, having espied but a glimpse of that eternal glory on the Mount, wished that he might dwell there all the days of his life, saying, «Master, it is good for us to be here.» (Mt. 17:4) How much better does Peter now think it to be in heaven itself! Christ, a little before his death, prays his Father to receive him into that excellent glory (Jn. 17:5). And the apostle witnesses, that «for the joy that was set before him, he endured the cross, and despised the shame.» Heb. 11:2. If a man did but once see those heavenly joys (if it were possible), he would endure an hundred deaths to enjoy that happiness but one day.

Augustine says, that he would be content to endure the torments of hell to gain this joy, rather than to lose it. Ignatius, Paul›s scholar, being threatened, as he was going to suffer, with the cruelty of torments, answered, with great courage of faith, «Fire, gallows, beasts, breaking of my bones, quartering of my members, crushing of my body, all the torments of the devil together—let them come upon me, so I may enjoy my Lord Jesus, and his kingdom.» The like constancy showed Polycarp, who could not by any terrors of any kind of death, be moved to deny Christ in the least measure. With the like resolution Basil answered his persecutors, when they would terrify him with death—»I will never,» said he, «fear death, which can do no more than restore me to him that made me.»

If Ruth left her own country, and followed Naomi, her mother-in-law, to go and dwell with her in the land of Canaan (which was but a type of heaven), only upon the fame which she heard of the God of Israel (though she had no promise of any portion in it), how should you follow Christ into the heavenly Canaan, where God has given you an eternal inheritance, assured by an holy covenant, made in the word of God, signed with the blood of his Son, and sealed with his Spirit and sacraments! This shall be your eternal happiness in the kingdom of heaven, where your **life** shall be a communion with the blessed Trinity; your **joy**, the presence of the Lamb; your **exercise**, singing; your **song**, hallelujah; your **companions**, saints and angels—where youth flourishes—and never becomes old; where beauty lasts—and never fades; where love abounds—and never cools; where health continues—and never slacks; and life remains—and never ends!

Meditations directing a Christian how to apply to himself without delay, based on the above knowledge of God and himself.

You see, therefore, O man, how wretched and cursed your state is, by corruption of nature, without Christ! Insomuch, that as the scriptures liken wicked men to lions, bears, bulls, horses, dogs, and such like savage creatures, in their lives—it is certain that the condition of an unregenerate man is in his death more vile than a dog, or the filthiest creature in the world. For the beast, being made but for man's use, when he dies, ends all his miseries with his death; but man, endued with a reasonable and an immortal soul, made after God's image, to serve God, when he ends the miseries of this life, must account for all his misdeeds, and begin to endure those miseries that never shall know end. No creature but man is responsible to yield at his death—an account for his life. The brute creatures, not having reason, shall not be required to make any account for their deeds—and good angels, though they have reason, yet shall they yield no account, because they have no sin. And as for evil angels, they are without all hope already condemned, so that they need not make any further accounts—man only in his death must be God's accountant for his life.

On the other side you see, O man, how happy and blessed your state is, being truly reconciled to God in Christ; in that, through the restoration of God's image, and your restitution into your sovereignty over other creatures, you are in this life little inferior to the angels, and shall be in the life to come equal to the angels— yes, in respect of your nature, exalted by a personal union to the Son of God, and by him to the glory of the Trinity, superior to the angels, a fellow-brother with angels in spiritual grace and everlasting glory.

You have seen how glorious and perfect God is, and how that all your chief bliss and happiness consists in having an eternal communion with him.

Now, therefore, O impenitent sinner! in the affections of Christ Jesus I entreat you, nay, I implore you, as you desire your own salvation, seriously to consider with me, how false, how vain, how vile—are those things which still retain and chain you in this wretched and cursed state wherein you live, and which hinder you from the favor of God, and the hope of eternal life and happiness!

MEDITATIONS FOR THE SICK

While your sickness remains, use often, for your comfort, these few meditations, taken from the ends why God sends afflictions to his children. Those are ten.

1. That by afflictions God may not only correct our sins past, but also work in us a deeper loathing of our natural corruptions, and so prevent us from falling into many other sins, which otherwise we would commit; like a good father, who allows his tender babe to scorch his finger in a candle, that he may the rather learn to beware of falling into a greater fire: so the child of God may say with David, "It is good for me that I have been afflicted, that I may learn your statutes; for before I was afflicted I went astray, but now I keep your word." And indeed, says Paul (1 Cor 11:32), "We are chastened by the Lord, because we should not be condemned with the world."

With one cross God makes two cures—the chastisement of sins past, and the prevention of sin to come. For though the eternal punishment of sin, as it proceeds from justice, is fully pardoned in the sacrifice of Christ, yet we are not, without serious judging ourselves, exempted from **the temporal chastisement of sin; for this proceeds only from the love of God, for our good**. And this is the reason, that when Nathan told David, from the Lord, that his sins were forgiven, yet that the sword of chastisement should not depart from his house, and that his child would surely die. For God, like a skillful physician, seeing the soul to be poisoned with the settling of sin, and knowing that the reigning of the flesh will prove the ruin of the Spirit, ministers **the bitter pill of affliction**, whereby the remains of sin are purged, and the soul more soundly cured; the flesh is subdued, and the spirit is sanctified. O the odiousness of sin, which causes God to chasten so severely his children, whom otherwise he loves so dearly!

2. God sends affliction to seal unto us our adoption, for "the Lord disciplines those he loves, and he punishes everyone he accepts as a son. Endure hardship as discipline; God is treating you as sons. For what son is not disciplined by his father? If you are not disciplined (and everyone undergoes discipline), then you are illegitimate children and not true sons." (Heb 12:6-8) Yes, it is a sure note, that where God sees sin and smites not, there he detests

and loves not; therefore it is said, that he allowed the wicked sons of Eli to continue in their sins, without correction, "because the Lord would slay them." On the other side, there is no surer token of God's fatherly love and care, than to be corrected with some cross, as often as we commit any sinful crime. Affliction, therefore, is a seal of adoption, no sign of reprobation; for the purest corn is cleanest fanned, the finest gold is most often tried, the sweetest grape is hardest pressed, and the truest Christian heaviest crossed.

3. God sends affliction to wean our hearts from too much loving this world and worldly vanities; and to cause us the more earnestly to desire and long for eternal life. As the children of Israel, had they not been ill-entreated in Egypt, would never have been so willing to go towards Canaan; so, were it not for the crosses and afflictions of this life, God's children would not so heartily long for and willingly desire the kingdom of heaven. For we see many epicures that would be content to forego heaven, on condition that they might still enjoy their earthly pleasures; and, having never tasted the joys of a better, how loath are they to depart this life? whereas the Apostle who saw heaven's glory tells us, that there is no more comparison between the joys of eternal life, and the pleasures of this world, than there is between the filthiest dung and the pleasantest food; or between the most noisome ash-heap and the fairest bedchamber (2 Cor 12:4; Phil 3:8)

God mixes sometimes affliction with the pleasures and prosperity of this life, lest, like the children of this generation, they should forget God, and fall into too much love of this present evil world; and so by riches grow proud; by fame, insolent; by liberty, wanton; and spurn with their heel against the Lord, when they wax fat (Deut 32:15) For if God's children love the world so well, when it misuses and strikes us; how would we love this harlot, if she smiled upon us, and stroked us, as she does her own worldly brats? Thus does God, like a wise and a loving father, embitter with crosses the pleasures of this life to his children, that, finding in this earthly state no true and permanent joys, they might sigh and long for eternal life, where firm and everlasting joys are only to be found.

4. By affliction and sickness God exercises his children, and the graces which he bestows upon them. He refines and tries their faith, as the goldsmith does his gold in the furnace--to make it shine more glistening and brightly (1 Pet 1:7) he stirs us up to pray more diligently, and zealously, and proves what patience we have

learned all this while in his school of affliction. The like experience he makes of our hope, love, and all the rest of our Christian virtues; which, without this trial, would rust, like iron; or corrupt like standing waters, which either have no current, or else are not poured from vessel to vessel; whose taste remains, and whose scent is not changed (Jer 48:11) And rather than a man should keep still the scent of his corrupt nature to damnation, who would not wish to be changed from state to state, by crosses and sickness, to salvation? For as the chamomile which is trodden grows best, and smells most fragrant; and as the fish is sweetest that lives in the saltest waters: so those souls are most precious to Christ who are most exercised and afflicted with crosses.

5. God sends afflictions, to demonstrate to the world the trueness of his children's love and service. Every hypocrite will serve God while he prospers and blesses him, as the devil falsely accused Job to have done: but who (but his loving child) will love and serve him in adversity, when God seems to be angry and displeased with him? yes, and cleave unto him most inseparably, when he seems with the greatest frown and disgrace to reject a man, and to cast him out of his favor; yes, when he seems to wound and kill as an enemy: yet, then to say with Job, "Though you, Lord, kill me, yet will I put my trust in you." The loving and the serving of God, and trusting in his mercy in the time of our correction and misery, is the truest note of a sincere child and servant of the Lord.

6. Sanctified affliction is a singular help to further our true conversion, and to drive us home by repentance to our heavenly Father. "In their affliction," says the Lord, "they will seek me diligently." (Hos 5:15) Egypt's burdens made Israel cry unto God (Exod 3:7) David's troubles made him pray (Psalm 86:7) Hezekiah's sickness made him weep (Isa 38:2-3;) and misery drove the prodigal child to return and plead for his father's grace and mercy. Yes, we read of many in the gospel, that by sicknesses and afflictions were driven to come unto Christ, who, if they had had health and prosperity as others, would have like others neglected or despised their Savior, and never have sought unto him for his saving health and grace. For as the ark of Noah, the higher it was tossed with the flood, the nearer it mounted towards heaven, so the sanctified soul, the more it is exercised with affliction, the nearer it is lifted towards God. O blessed is that cross which draws a sinner to come upon the knees of his heart unto Christ, to confess his own misery, and to implore his endless mercy! O blessed, ever blessed be that Christ, that never refuses the sinner that comes unto him,

though weather-driven by affliction and misery!

7. Affliction works in us pity and compassion toward our fellow-brethren that are in distress and misery; whereby we learn to have a fellow-feeling of their calamities, and to condole their estate, as if we suffered with them (Heb 13:3) And for this cause Christ himself would suffer, and be tempted in all things like unto us (sin only excepted) that he might be a merciful High Priest, touched with the feeling of our infirmities (Heb 4:15; Heb 2:18; Heb 5:8-9) For none can so heartily bemoan the misery of another, as he who first himself suffered the same affliction. Hereupon a sinner in misery may boldly say to Christ.

8. God uses our sicknesses and afflictions as means and examples both to manifest to others the faith and virtues which he has bestowed upon us, as also to strengthen those who have not received so great a measure of faith as we; for there can be no greater encouragement to a weak Christian, than to behold a true Christian in the extreme sickness of his body, supported with greater patience and consolation in his soul. And the comfortable and blessed departure of such a man will arm him against the fear of death, and assure him that the hope of the godly is a far more precious thing than that flesh and blood can understand, or mortal eyes behold, in this valley of misery. And were it not that we did see many of those whom we know to be the undoubted children of God, to have endured such afflictions and calamities before us, the greatness of the miseries and crosses which ofttimes we endure, would make us doubt whether we are the children of God or not. And to this purpose James says, "God made Job and the prophets an example of suffering adversity, and of long patience."

9. By afflictions God makes us conformable to the image of Christ his Son (Rom 8:18; 1 Pet 4:14), who being the captain of our salvation, was made perfect through sufferings (Heb 2:10) And therefore he first bore the cross in shame, before he was crowned with glory (Heb 2:7) did first take gall (Matt 27:34), before he did eat the honeycomb (Luke 24:42;) and was derided King of the Jews, by the soldiers in the High Priest's hall, before he was saluted King of glory, by the angels in his Father's court (Psalm 24:7) And the more lively our heavenly Father shall perceive the image of his natural Son to appear in us, the better he will love us; and when we have for a time borne his likeness in his sufferings, and fought (2 Tim 4:7-8) and overcome (Rev 3:21), we shall be crowned by Christ; and with Christ, sit on his throne; and from Christ receive the precious white stone and morning-star (Rev 2:17), that shall

make us shine like Christ forever in his glory (Phil 3:21)

10. Lastly, that the godly may be humbled in respect of their own state and misery; and God glorified by delivering them out of their troubles and afflictions, when they call upon him for his help and support. For though there be no man so pure, but if the Lord will straitly mark iniquities he shall find in him just cause to punish him for his sin; yet the Lord in mercy does not always, in the affliction of his children, respect their sins, but sometimes lays afflictions and crosses upon them for his glory's sake. Thus our Savior Christ told his disciples, that the man was not born blind for his own or his parents' sin, but that the work of God should be showed on him. So he told them likewise that Lazarus's sickness was not unto the death, but for the glory of God. O the unspeakable goodness of God, which turns those afflictions, which are the shame and punishment due to our sins, to be the subject of his honor and glory!

These are the blessed and profitable ends for which God sends sickness and affliction upon his children; whereby it may plainly appear that afflictions are not signs either of God's hatred or our reprobation; but rather tokens and pledges of his fatherly love unto children whom he loves, and therefore chastens them in this life, where, upon repentance, there remains hope of pardon; rather than to refer the punishment to that life where there is no hope of pardon, nor end of punishment. For this cause, the Christians in the primitive church were accustomed to give God great thanks for afflicting them in this life. So the apostles rejoiced, that they were counted worthy to suffer for Christ's name (Acts 5:41) And the Christian Hebrews suffered with joy the confiscation of their goods, knowing that they had in heaven a better, and an enduring substance (Heb 10:34)

And in respect of those holy ends, the apostle says, "that though no affliction for the present seems joyous, but grievous; yet afterwards it brings the quiet fruit of righteousness to them who are exercised thereby." (Heb 12:11) Pray, therefore, heartily, that as God has sent you this sickness, so it would please him to come himself unto you with your sickness, by teaching you to make those sanctified uses of it, for which he has inflicted the same upon you.

CONSOLATIONS AGAINST IMPATIENCE IN SICKNESS

If in your sickness by extremity of pain you be driven to impatience, meditate—

1. That your sins have deserved the pains of hell; therefore you may with greater patience endure these fatherly corrections.

2. That these are the scourges of your heavenly Father, and the rod is in his hand. If you did suffer with reverence, being a child, the corrections of your earthly parents, how much rather should you now subject yourself, being the child of God, to the chastisement of your heavenly Father, seeing it is for your eternal good?

3. That Christ suffered in his soul and body far more grievous pains for you, therefore you must more willingly suffer his blessed pleasure for your own good (Isa 53:3) Therefore, says Peter, "Christ suffered for you, leaving you an example that you should follow his steps" (1 Pet 2:21) And "Let us," says Paul, "run with joy the race that is set before us, looking unto Jesus the author and finisher of our faith, who for the joy that was set before him, endured the cross," etc. (Heb 12:1-2)

4. That these afflictions which now you suffer are none other but such as "are accomplished in your brethren that are in the world," as witnesses Peter (1 Pet 5:9;) yes, Job's afflictions were far more grievous. There is not one of the saints which now are at rest in heavenly joys, but endured as much as you do before they went there; yes, many of them willingly suffered all the torments that tyrants could inflict upon them, that they might come unto those heavenly joys to which you are now called. And you have a promise, that "the God of all grace, after you have suffered a while, will make you perfect, establish, strengthen, and settle you" (1 Pet 5:10)

5. That God has determined the time when your affliction shall end, as well as the time when it began. Thirty-eight years were appointed the sick man at the pool of Bethesda (John 5:5) Twelve years to the woman who was suffering from bleeding (Matt 9:20) Three months to Moses (Exod 2:2) Ten days' tribulation to the angel of the Church at Smyrna (Rev 2:10) Three days plague to David (2 Sam 24:13) Yes, the number of the godly man's tears

are registered in God's book--and the quantity kept in his bottle (Psalm 56:8)

The time of our trouble, says Christ, is but a little while (John 16:16) God's anger lasts but a moment, says David (Psalm 30) A little season, says the Lord (Rev 6:11) and therefore calls all the time of our pain but the *hour* of sorrow (John 16:21) David, for the swiftness of it, compares our present trouble to a brook (Psalm 110:7), and Athanasius to a shower. **Compare the longest misery that man endures in this life--to the eternity of heavenly joys; and they will appear to be nothing!** "For I consider that the sufferings of this present time are not worth comparing with the glory that is going to be revealed to us." (Romans 8:18) And as the sight of a son safely born, makes the mother forget all her former deadly pain (John 16:21), so the sight of Christ in heaven, who was born for you, will make all these pangs of death to be quite forgotten, as if they had never been. Like Stephen, who, as soon as he saw Christ, forgot his own wounds, with the horror of the grave, and terror of the stones, and sweetly yielded his soul into the hands of his Savior (Acts 7) Forget your own pain, think of Christ's wounds. Be faithful unto the death, and he will give you the crown of eternal life (Rev 2:10)

6. That you are now called to repetitions in Christ's school of affliction, to see how much faith, patience, and godliness, you have learned all this while; and whether you can, like Job, receive at the hand of God some evil, as well as you have hitherto received a great deal of good (Job 2:10) As therefore you have always prayed, "Your will be done," so be not now offended at this which is done by his holy will.

7. That "all things shall work together for the best, to those who love God;" insomuch that "neither death, nor life, nor angels, nor principalities, nor powers, etc., shall be able to separate us from the love of God which is in Christ Jesus our Lord." (Rom 8:28,38-39) Assure yourself that every pang is a prevention of the pains of hell, every respite a pledge of heaven's rest; and how many stripes do you esteem heaven worth? As your life has been a comfort to others, so give your friends a Christian example to die. Death is but the cross of Christ sent before to crucify the love of the world in you, that you may go eternally to live with Christ who was crucified for you. As you are therefore a true Christian, take up, like Simeon of Cyrene, with both your arms, his holy cross, carry it after him unto him. Your pains will shortly pass, your joys shall never pass away.

MEDITATIONS FOR ONE
WHO IS LIKELY TO DIE

If your sickness be like to increase unto death, then meditate on three things:

First, How graciously God deals with you.

Secondly, From what evils death will free you.

Thirdly, What good death will bring unto you.

The first sort of Meditations are, to **consider God's favorable dealing with you**.

1. Meditate that God uses this chastisement of your body but as a medicine to cure your soul, by drawing you, who are sick in sin, to come by repentance unto Christ, your physician, to have your soul healed (Matt 9:12)

2. That the sorest sickness or most painful disease which you can endure, is nothing, if it is compared to those dolours and pains which Jesus Christ your Savior has suffered for you, when in a bloody sweat he endured the wrath of God (Psalm 88:7; Isa 53:6), the pains of hell (Psalm 18:5), and a cursed death which was due to your sins (Heb 5:7; Gal 3:13; Lam 1:12) Justly, therefore, may he use those words of Jeremiah, "Behold, and see if there be any sorrow like unto my sorrow which is done unto me, with which the Lord has afflicted me in the day of his fierce wrath." Has the Son of God endured so much for your redemption, and will not you, a sinful man, endure a little sickness for his pleasure, especially when it is for your good?

3. That when your sickness and disease is at the extreme, yet it is less and easier than your sins have deserved. Let your own conscience judge whether you have not deserved worse than all that you do suffer. Murmur not, therefore, but considering your manifold and grievous sins; thank God that you are not plagued with far more grievous punishments. Think how willingly the damned in hell would endure your extreme pains for a thousand years, on condition that they had but the hope to be saved, and, after so many years, to be eased of their eternal torments. And seeing that it is his mercy that you are corrected, rather than consumed (Lam 3:22), how can you but bear patiently his temporal correction, seeing the end is to save you from eternal condemnation? (1

Cor 11:32)

4. That nothing comes to pass in this case unto you but such as ordinarily befell others your brethren; who, being the beloved and undoubted servants of God when they lived on earth (Heb 11), are now most blessed and glorious saints with Christ in heaven, as Job, David, Lazarus, etc. (1 Pet 5:9) They groaned for a time, as you do, under the like burden; but they are now delivered from all their miseries, troubles, and calamities. And so likewise before long, if you will patiently tarry the Lord's leisure, you shall also be delivered from your sickness and pain; either by restitution to your former health with Job; or, which is far better, by being received to heavenly rest with Lazarus.

5. Lastly, That God has not given you over into the hand of your enemy to be punished and disgraced; but, being your loving Father, he corrects you with his own merciful hand. When David had his wish to choose his own chastisement, he chose rather to be corrected by the hand of God than by any other means: "Let us fall into the hand of the Lord, for his mercies are great; and let me not fall into the hand of man." (2 Sam 24:14) Who will not take any affliction in good part when it comes from the hand of God, from whom, though no affliction seems joyous for the present, we know nothing comes but what is good? (Heb 12:11) The consideration of which made David endure Shimei's cursed railing with greater patience; and to correct himself another time for his impatience (2 Sam 16:9), "I should not have opened my mouth, because God is the one who has done this." (Psalm 39:9) and Job, to reprove the unadvised speech of his wife, "You speak like a foolish woman. What! shall we receive good at the hand of God, and not receive evil?" (Job 2:10) And though the cup of God's wrath due to our sins, was such a horror to our Savior's human nature that he earnestly prayed that it might pass from him, yet, when he considered that it was reached unto him by the hand and will of his Father, he willingly submitted himself to drink it to the very dregs (Matt 26:39,42) Nothing will more arm you with patience in your sickness, than to see that it comes from the hand of your heavenly Father, who would never send it but that he sees it to be to you both needful and profitable.

The second sort of Meditations are, to **consider from what evils Death will free you**.

1. It frees you from a corruptible body, which was conceived in the weakness of flesh; and the stain of sin—a living prison of your soul, a lively instrument of sin. Insomuch, that whereas trees and

plants bring forth leaves, flowers, fruits, and sweet fragrances, man's body naturally brings forth nothing but corruption. His affections are altogether corrupted (Psalm 14:1;) and the imaginations of his heart are only evil continually (Gen 6:5) Hence it is that the ungodly is not satisfied with profaneness, nor the voluptuous with pleasures, nor the ambitious with advancements, nor the malicious with revenge, nor the lewd with uncleanness, nor the covetous with gain, nor the drunkard with drinking. New passions and fashions grow daily; new fears and afflictions still arise: here wrath lies in wait, there vainglory vexes; here pride lifts up, there disgrace casts down; and everyone waits what shall arise on the ruin of another. Now a man is privily stung with backbiters, like fiery serpents; anon he is in danger to be openly devoured by his enemies, like Daniel's lions. And a godly man, wherever he lives, shall ever be vexed, like Lot, with Sodom's uncleanness.

2. Death brings to the godly an end of sinning (Rom 6:7), and of all the miseries which are due to sin; so that after death, "there shall be no more sorrow nor crying; neither shall there be any more pain; for God shall wipe away all tears from their eyes." (Rev 21:4) Yes, by death we are separated from the company of wicked men; and God "takes away merciful and righteous men from the evil to come." (Isa 57:1) So he dealt with Josiah: "I will gather you to your fathers, and you shall be put into your grave in peace; and your eyes shall not see all the evil which I will bring unto this place." (2 Kings 22:20) And God "hides them for a while in the grave, until the indignation passes over." (Isa 26:20) So that as paradise is the haven of the soul's joy, so the grave may be termed the haven of the body's rest.

3. Whereas this wicked body lives in a world of wickedness, so that the poor soul cannot look out at the eye, and not be infected; nor hear by the ear, and not be distracted; nor smell at the nostrils, and not be tainted; nor taste with the tongue, and not be allured; nor touch by the hand, and not be defiled; and every sense, upon every temptation, is ready to betray the soul: By death the soul shall be delivered from this thraldom; and this "corruptible body shall put on incorruption, and this mortal immortality." (1 Cor 15:53) O blessed, thrice blessed be that death in the Lord, which delivers us out of so evil a world, and frees us from such a body of bondage and corruption!

The third sort of Meditations are, to consider **what good Death will bring unto you**.

1. Death brings the godly man's soul to enjoy an immediate com-

munion with the blessed Trinity, in everlasting bliss and glory.

2. It translates the soul from the miseries of this world, the contagion of sin, and society of sinners--to the "city of the living God, the celestial Jerusalem, and the company of innumerable angels, and to the assembly and congregation of the firstborn, which are written in heaven, and to God the Judge of all, and to the souls of just men made perfect, and to Jesus, the mediator of the new covenant." (Heb 12:22-24)

3. Death puts the soul into the actual and full possession of all the inheritance and happiness which Christ has either promised to you in his word, or purchased for you by his blood.

This is the good and happiness to which a blessed death will bring you. And what truly pious Christian who is young, would not wish himself old, that his appointed time might the sooner approach, to enter into this celestial paradise? where you may exchange your brass for gold, your vanity for felicity, your vileness for honor, your bondage for freedom, your lease for an inheritance, and your mortal state for an immortal life. He who does not daily desire this blessedness above all things, of all others he is less worthy to enjoy it.

If Cato Uticensis, and Cleombrotus, two heathen men, reading Plato's book of the immortality of the soul, did voluntarily, the one break his neck, the other run upon his sword, that they might the sooner, as they thought, have enjoyed those joys; what a shame it is for Christians, knowing those things in a more excellent measure and manner out of God's own book, not to be willing to enter into these heavenly joys, especially when their Master calls for them there? (Matt 25:21) If, therefore, there is in you any love of God, or desire of your own happiness or salvation, when the time of your departing draws near—that time, I say, and manner of death, which God in his unchangeable counsel has appointed and determined before you were born—yield and surrender up willingly and cheerfully your soul into the merciful hands of Jesus Christ your Savior.

CONSOLATIONS AGAINST
THE FEAR OF DEATH

If in the time of your sickness you find yourself fearful to die,
meditate—

1. That it argues a weak mind, to fear that which is not; for
there is no death for Christians (Isa 25:7-8). Whoever believes in
Christ, shall never die (John 11:26). Let them fear death, who live
without Christ. Christians do not die; but when they please God,
they are like Enoch translated unto God (Gen 5:24;) their pains
are but Elijah's fiery chariot to carry them up to heaven (2 Kings
2:11-12;) or like the sores of Lazarus sending them to Abraham's
bosom (Luke 16:23) In a word, if you are one of those who, like
Lazarus, love Jesus, your sickness is not unto the death, but for
the glory of God (John 11:4), who of his love changes your living
death to an everlasting life. And if many heathen men, as Socrates,
Curtius, Seneca, etc., died willingly, when they might have lived,
in hope of the immortality of the soul; will you, being trained so
long in Christ's school, and now called to the marriage-supper of
the blessed Lamb (Rev 19:7), be one of those guests who refuse to
go to that joyful banquet? God forbid!

**2. Remember that your abode here is but the second stage of
your life**; for after you had first lived nine months in your mother's womb, you were of necessity driven thence to live here in a
second stage of life. And when that number of months which God
has determined for this life has expired (Job 14:5), you must likewise leave this and pass to a third stage in the other world, which
never ends; which, to those who live and die in the Lord, surpass-
es as far this kind of life as this does that stage which one lives in
his mother's womb. To this last and most excellent degree of life,
through this door passed Christ himself, and all his saints who
were before you; and so shall all the rest after you. Why should
you fear that which is common to all God's elect? why should that
be unwelcome to you, which was so welcome to all them? Fear not
death, for as it is the exodus of an evil world--so it is the genesis
of a better world; the end of a temporal life--but the beginning of
an eternal life.

3. Consider that there are but three things that can make

death so fearful to you:

First, The loss you have thereby;

Secondly, The pain that is therein;

Thirdly, The terrible effects which follow after.

All these are but false fires and causeless fears.

For the first, If you leave here uncertain goods--which thieves may rob; you shall find in heaven a true treasure--which can never be taken away (Matt 6:19-20) These were but lent you as a steward upon accounts--those shall be given you as your reward forever. If you leave a loving wife, you shall be married to Christ, which is more lovely. If you leave children and friends, you shall there find all your pious ancestors—yes, Christ, and all his blessed saints and angels; and as many of your children as are God's children, shall there follow after you. You leave an earthly possession and a house of clay (2 Cor 5:1), and you shall enjoy an heavenly inheritance and mansion of glory, which is purchased, prepared, and reserved for you (John 14:2) What have you lost? Nay, is not death unto you gain? Go home, go home, and we will follow after you.

Secondly, For the pain in death. The fear of death more pains many, than the very pangs of death; for many a Christian dies without any great pangs or pains. Pitch the anchor of your hope on the firm ground of the word of God, who has promised in your weakness to perfect his strength (2 Cor 12:9), and Christ will shortly turn all your temporal pains to his eternal joys.

Lastly, As for the terrible effects which follow after death, they belong not unto you, being a member of Christ; for Christ by his death has taken away the sting of death to the faithful, so that now there is no condemnation to those who are in Christ Jesus (Rom 8:1) And Christ has protested, that he who believes in him has everlasting life, and shall not come into condemnation, but has passed from death unto life (John 5:24) Upon which the Holy Spirit from heaven says, "Blessed are the dead who die in the Lord; and that from henceforth they rest from their labors and their works do follow them." In respect, therefore, of the faithful, death is swallowed up in victory, and its sting, which is sin and the punishment of it--is taken away by Christ (1 Cor 15:54) Hence death is called, in respect of our bodies, a sleep and rest (1 Thess 4:13; Isa 26; Rev 14;) in respect of our souls, a going to our heavenly Father, a departing in peace, a removing from this body to go to the Lord, a dissolution of soul and body to be with Christ.

What shall I say? "Precious in the sight of the Lord is the death of his saints." These pains are but your throes and travail to bring forth eternal life. And who would not pass through hell, to go to paradise? much more through death. There is nothing after death that you need fear; not your sins, because Christ has paid your ransom; not the Judge, for he is your loving brother; not the grave, for it is the Lord's bed; not hell, for your Redeemer keeps the keys; not the devil, for God's holy angels pitch their tents about you, and will not leave you until they bring you to heaven. You were never nearer eternal life; glorify, therefore, Christ by a blessed death. Say cheerfully, "Come, Lord Jesus, for your servant comes unto you. I am willing, Lord help my weakness."

DIRECTIONS FOR COMFORTABLE WALKING WITH GOD

"But **Noah** found favor in the eyes of the Lord. Noah was a righteous man, blameless in his generations. Noah walked with God." (Genesis 6:8-9)

In this dreadful and dismal story of the old world's degeneracy and destruction, falling away, and final ruin—here stands in my text a radiant and illustrious star, shining lovely with singularity of heavenly light, spiritual goodness, and God's sincere service, in the darkest midnight of Satan's universal reign, and amidst the strangest confusions, idolatrous corruptions, cruelties, oppressions, and lust—which ever the earth bore. **Noah**, a very precious man, and preacher of righteousness, and his family, were alone excepted. The true worship of God was confined to them, when all the world besides lay drowned in idolatry and paganism, ready to be swallowed up in a universal grave of waters, which was already fashioned in the clouds by the angry, irresistible hand of the all-powerful God, who was now so implacably—but most justly, provoked by those rebellious and cruel generations, that he would not allow his Spirit to strive any more with them; but inexorably resolved to open the windows or floodgates of heaven, giving extraordinary strength of influence above, and abundance to the fountains of the great deep, commanding them to cast out the whole treasure and heap of their waters; and taking away the retentive power from the clouds, that they might pour down immeasurably, for the burying of all living creatures which breathed in the air. From whence, by the way, before I break into my text, take this note.

Doctrine. The servants of God are men of singularity. I mean it not in respect of any fantasticalness of opinion, furiousness of zeal, or turbulence of faction, truly so called; but in respect of abstinence from sin, purity of heart, and holiness of life.

REASONS.

1. God's holy word exacts and expects from all that are born again, and heirs of heaven, an excellency above ordinary, Prov. 12:26; Matt. 5:20, 41. Being taken forth as the precious from the vile, Jer. 15:19, by the power of the ministry, they must not only

go beyond the highest civil perfections of the exact moral purity among the most honest heathens, Heb. 12:14—but also exceed the righteousness and all the outward religious conformities of the most devout pharisees, who many thousands in these times come short of, and yet hope to be saved: or they can in no case enter into the kingdom of heaven. But, lest any be proudly puffed up with a sense of this singularity and excellency above his neighbor, let him know that **humility** is ever one of the fairest flowers in the whole garland of supernatural and divine worth; and that self-conceit would poison even angelical perfection.

2. They must upon necessity differ from a world of wicked men, by a sincere singularity of abstinence from the course of this world, the lusts of men, the corruptions of the times, familiarity with graceless companions, the worldling's language, profane sports, all wicked ways of thriving, rising, and growing great in the world, and so forth.

3. They make conscience of those duties and Divine commands, which the greatest part of men, even in the noontide of the gospel, are so far from taking to heart, that their hearts rise against them. As, to be warm in religion, Rev. 3:16; to be zealous of good works, Tit. 2:14; to walk precisely, Eph. 5:15; to be fervent in spirit, Rom. 12:11; to strive to enter in at the strait gate, Luke 13:24; to pluck out their right eyes; that is, to abandon their bosom delights, Matt. 5:29; to make the sabbath a delight, Isa. 53:13; to love the brotherhood, 1 Pet. 2:11; with a holy violence to lay hold upon the kingdom of heaven, Matt. 11:12.

4. Experience, and examples of all ages, from the creation downward, clearly prove the point. At this time, as you see, the saints of God were all harbored under one roof, and yet not all sound there. Survey the ages afterward—the time of Abraham, who was as a brand taken out of the fire of the Chaldeans; the time of Elijah, when none appeared to that blessed man of God; the time of Isaiah, who cried, "Who has believed our report?" chapter 53:1; the time of Manasseh, who built altars for all the army of heaven, in the two courts of the house of the Lord; the time of Antiochus, when he commanded the sanctuary and holy people to be polluted with swine's flesh, and unclean beasts to be sacrificed, the abomination of desolation to be set up upon the altar; that darksome time when the glorious Day-star, Christ Jesus himself, came down from heaven to enlighten the earth; the time of Antichrist, when all the world wondered after the beast; our times, wherein, of six parts of the earth, probably scarce one of the least is Christian.

And how much of Christendom is still overgrown with popery, and other exorbitant distempers in point of religion. And where the truth of Christ is purely and powerfully taught, how few give their names unto it! and of those who profess, how many are false-hearted, or merely formal.

5. Methinks worldly wisdom should rather wonder that any one is won unto God, than cry out and complain, Is it possible there should be so few? since all the powers of darkness, and every devil in hell, oppose, might and main, the implanting of grace in any soul; since there are more snares upon earth to keep us still in the invisible chains of darkness and sin, than there are stars in heaven; since every inch, every little artery of our bodies, if it could, would swell with hellish venom to the bigness of the great-est Goliath, the mightiest giant, that it might make resistance to the sanctifying work of the Holy Spirit; since our souls, naturally, would rather die and put off their immortality and everlasting be-ing, than put on the Lord Jesus—in a word, since the new creation of a man is held to be a greater work of wonder than the creation of the world.

6. Let us set aside in any country, city, town, family:

First, all atheists, papists, and distempered heretics—from the blessed truth of doctrine taught in our church.

Secondly, all whoremongers, drunkards, swearers, liars, revel-ers, worldlings, unjust, and fellows of such infamous rank.

Thirdly, all merely civil men, who come short of other honest heathens, and, lacking holiness, shall never see the Lord, Heb. 12:14.

Fourthly, all gross hypocrites, whose outsides are painted with superficial flourishes of holiness and honesty—but their inward parts filled with rottenness and lust, who have their hands in god-ly exercises, when their hearts are in hell.

Fifthly, all formal hypocrites, who are deluded in point of salva-tion, as were the foolish virgins, and that proud pharisee, Luke 18:11.

Sixthly, all final backsliders, of which some turn sensual epi-cures, and plunge themselves into worldly pleasures with far more rage and greediness, by reason of former restraint by a tempo-rary profession; others become scurrilous deriders of the holy way; some, bloody goads into the sides of those with whom they have formerly walked into the house of God as friends.

Seventhly, all unsound professors for the present, of which you would little think what a number there is.

I say, let these and all other strangers to the purity and power of godliness be set apart, and tell me how many true-hearted Nathaniels we are likely to find.

USES—

1. Try then the truth of your spiritual state by this mark of a sober and sincere singularity. If you still hold correspondence with the world, and conform to the fashions thereof, if still you swim down the current of the times, and shift your sails to the turn of every wind; if your heart still hankers after the tasteless fooleries of the popular, and follow the multitude to do evil; if you are carried with the swing and sway of the place where you live, to uphold, by a boisterous combination, lewdness and vanity, to scorn profession, oppose the ministry, and walk in the broad way. In a word, if you do as the most do, you are utterly undone forever.

But if with a merciful violence you are pulled out of the world by the power of the word, and happily weaned from the sensual, insensible poison of all bittersweet pleasures, and fellowship with unfruitful works of darkness; if, by standing on God's side, and hatred of all false ways, you have become the drunkard's song, as David was, and a by-word among the sons of Belial, as was Job; if the world lowers and looks sour upon you for your looking towards heaven, and your fellows abandon you as too precise; if your life be not like other men's, and your ways of another fashion, as the epicures of those times charged the righteous man when the Book of Wisdom was written; in a word, if you walk in the narrow way, and be one of that little flock which lives among wolves, and therefore must needs be little; so that by all the leopards, lions, and bears about you, I mean all sorts of unregenerate men, you are hunted for your holiness as a partridge on the mountains, at least by the poison and persecution of the tongue—I say then you are certainly in the high way to heaven.

2. If the saints of God be men of singularity in the sense I have said, then away with those base and brainless cavils against those who are wise unto salvation. What! are you wiser than your forefathers? than all the town? than such and such learned men? than your own parents? Nay further, to Noah it might have been said by the wretches of those times—Are you wiser than all the world? He, out of the height of his heroical resolution, easily endured and digested the affronts and indignities of this kind from millions of men. But take these spiteful taunts, and bind them in the meantime as a crown unto you, and advance forward in your holy singularity with all sweet content and undauntedness of spirit,

towards that glorious immortal crown above; and let those miserable men, whose eyes are hoodwinked by Satan, and so blinded with earthly dust that they cannot possibly discern the invisible excellences and true nobleness of the neglected saints, follow the folly of their worldly wisdom, and sway of the greater part, to endless woe, and then give believers leave to talk.

3. Let everyone, who in sincerity of heart seeks to be saved, ever hold it a special happiness and his highest honor to be singled out from the universal pestilent contagion of common profaneness, and the sinful courses of the greatest part, and to be censured as singular in that respect. Neither is this a singular thing that I now suggest—but it has been the portion of the saints in all ages to be trod upon with the feet of imperious contempt, as a number of odd despised underlings; whereas indeed they are God's jewels, and the only excellent upon earth. "Behold," says Isaiah, chapter 8:18, "I and the children whom the Lord has given me are for signs and wonders in Israel." "I am as a wonder unto many," says David, Psalm 71:7. "I am in derision daily, everyone mocks me," says Jeremiah, chapter 20:7. "We are made," says Paul, "a spectacle unto the world, and to angels, and to men," 1 Cor. 4:9. "We are made as the filth of the earth, the off-scouring of all things," 4:13. In Augustine's time, those that made conscience of their ways, dared not plunge into the corruptions of the times, were scornfully pointed at, not only by pagans—but even by unreformed professors, professors at large as we call them, as fellows that affected a preciseness and purity above ordinary and other men—they would thus insult and scoffingly fly in the face of such a holy one, "You are a great man, sure you are a just man, you are an Elijah, you are a Peter, you come from heaven!"

In after times, if a man were but merely civil, ingenuous, chaste, temperate, he was made a by-word and laughing-stock to those about him. They presently said—He was proud, singular, beside himself, hypocrite, etc. Thus it was, is at this time, and will be to the world's end, that every vile whoremonger, beastly drunkard, ignorant scoundrel, scoffing Ishmael, and self-guilty wretch, will have a bitter sneer or reproach to throw, like the madman's firebrand, into the face of God's people, as though they were a company of nasty fellows, and a contemptible generation. This, I say, ever was and ever will be the world's opinion of the ways of God's people. The children of darkness ever harbor such conceits, and peremptorily pass such censures upon the children of light.

It is strange, men are content to be singular in anything but in the service of God, and the salvation of their souls! They desire, and labor too, to be singularly rich, and the wealthiest in a town; to be singularly proud, and in fashion by themselves; to be the strongest in the company to pour in strong drink. They would, with all their hearts, be in honor alone, and adored above others. They would dwell alone, and not allow a poor man's house to be within sight. They affect singularity in wit, learning, wisdom, valor, worldly reputation, and in all other earthly honors; but they can by no means endure a singularity in zeal and the Lord's service. In matters of religion they are resolved to do as the most do, though in so doing they certainly damn their own souls, Matt. 7:13. Basest cowardliness and fearfulness fit for such a doom! Rev. 21:8. They are afraid of taking God's part too much, of fighting too valiantly under the colors of Christ, of being too busy about the salvation of their souls, lest they should be accounted too precise, fellows of an odd humor, and engrossers of more grace than ordinary. It is one of Satan's dreadful depths, as wide as hell, and brim-full with the blood of immortal souls, to make men ambitious and covetous of singularity in all other things but in godliness and God's services—not to allow it in themselves, and to persecute it in others.

Now, in this story of **Noah**, so highly honored with singularity of freedom from the sinful contagion of those desperate times, and happily exempted from that most general and greatest judgment upon earth that ever the sun saw—a universal drowning—gloriously mounting up upon the wings of salvation, and safety both of soul and body, when a world of giant-like rebels sunk to the bottom of that new sea as a stone or lead, I consider,

1. The cause of such a singular blessed preservation, which was the free grace and favor of God; "But Noah found grace in the eyes of the Lord," 5:8.

2. The renown and honor of Noah's name; in that he stands here as the father of the new world, and the holy seed and progenitor of Jesus Christ; "These are the generations of Noah," ver. 9.

3. The description of Noah's personal goodness, preservation, and posterity. These latter two follow.

His personal description stands in the end of ver. 9; "Noah was a just man and perfect in his generations; and Noah walked with God," where we find him honored with three noble attributes, which make up the character of a complete Christian—honesty, uprightness, and piety. And they receive much excellency and luster from a circumstance of time; "In his generations," which were many and mainly corrupt.

I. The **CAUSE** of such a singular blessed preservation, which was the free grace and favor of God; "But Noah found **grace** in the eyes of the Lord," 5:8. **Preservation is of God's Free Grace**

Without any further unfolding my text's coherence and dependence upon either precedent or following parts, (for historical passages are plainer, and do not ever exact the length and labor of such an exact resolution as other Scriptures do,) I collect from the first point, wherein I find God's free grace to be the prime and principal cause of Noah's preservation, this

Doctrine. **The free grace and favor of God are the first mover and fountain of all our good.** Consider for this purpose such places as these—Jer. 31:3; Hos. 14:4; Deut. 7:7, 8; Rom. 9:11, 12, 13; John 3:16; Josh. 24:2, 3; Eph. 1:5.

And it must needs be so. For it is utterly impossible that any finite cause, created power, or anything out of God himself, should primarily move and incline the eternal, immutable, uncreated, omnipotent will of God. The true original and prime motive of all gracious, bountiful expressions and effusions of love upon his elect, is the good pleasure of his will. And therefore to hold that election to life is made upon foresight of faith, good works the right use of free will, or any created motive, is not only false and wicked—but also an ignorant and absurd tenet. To say no more at this time, it robs God of his all-sufficiency, making him go out of himself, looking to this or that in the creature, upon which his will may be determined to elect. The school-men, though otherwise a rotten generation of divines, yet are right in this.

Uses. 1. All praise then is due unto Jehovah, the Author of all our good, the Fountain of all our bliss, the Well-spring of immortality and life, "in whom we live and move, and have our being;" our natural being, the being of our outward state; our gracious being; the everlastingness of our glorious state. Were the holiest heart upon earth enlarged to the vast comprehension of this great world's wideness; nay, made capable of all the glorious and magnificent hallelujahs and hearty praises offered to Jehovah, both by all the militant and triumphant church, yet would it come infinitely short of sufficiently magnifying, admiring, and adoring the inexplicable mystery and bottomless depth of this free, independent mercy, and love of God, the Fountain and First Mover of all our good.

We may, and are bound to bless God for all the means, instruments, and second causes, whereby it pleases him to confer and convey good things unto us; but we must rest principally, with lowliest thoughts of most humble and hearty praisefulness, at the well head of all our welfare, Jehovah, blessed forever. We receive a great deal of comfort and light from the moon and stars—but we are chiefly indebted to the sun; from the greater rivers also—but the main sea is the fountain. Angels, ministers, and men may please us—but Jehovah is the principal. Let us then imitate those lights of heaven and rivers of the earth; do all the good we can with those good things God has given us by his instruments; and then reflect back towards, and return all the glory and praise unto, the Sun of righteousness and Sea of our salvation. The beams of the moon and stars return as far back to glorify the face of the sun, which gave them their beauty, as they can possibly; so let us ever send back to God's own glorious self the honor of all his gifts, by a fruitful improvement of them, in setting forth his glory, and by continual fervent ejaculations of praise to the utmost possibility of our renewed hearts.

And here I cannot forbear—but must needs most justly complain of the hateful, intolerable unthankfulness of us in this kingdom, the happiest people under the arch of heaven, had we hearts enlarged to conceive aright of God's extraordinary love, and such miraculous mercies as never any nation enjoyed. Walk over the world, peruse the whole face of the earth from east to west, from north to south, and from one side of heaven to another, you shall not find such another enlightened Goshen as this island wherein we dwell. Of six parts of the earth, five are not Christian; and in Christendom, what other part is so free from the reign of popery, the rage of schism, or the destroying sword? Or where besides does the gospel shine with such glory, truth, and peace? Or in what nook of the world are there so many faithful souls who cry unto God day and night against the abominations of the times, for the preservation of the gospel, that God's name may be gloriously hallowed, his kingdom come, his will be done in every place, and who themselves serve him with truth of heart?

And yet we are too ready, if we have not the height of our desires, and our wills to the full, instead of patience, tears, and prayers, which best become the saints, to embitter all other blessings, and to discover most horrible unthankfulness for them, by repining, grumbling, and discontent; by not rejoicing, as we ought, in every good thing which the Lord our God has given unto us, and by not improving the extraordinariness of his mercies to our more glorious service of him, and more humbly and precisely walking before him.

Away then with all sour, melancholy, causeless, sinful discontent; and "praise the Lord; sing unto the Lord a new song, and his praise in the congregation of the saints. Let Israel rejoice in him who made him—let the children of Zion be joyful in their King. For the Lord takes pleasure in his people—he will beautify the meek with salvation. Let the saints be joyful in glory—let them sing aloud upon their beds," Ps. 149:1, 2, 4, 5. In a word, let us of this island, as we have just cause above all the nations of the earth, and above all ages of the church, from the very first creation of it, praise Jehovah most heartily, infinitely, and forever.

2. Never reproach any for deformity of body, dullness of mind, weakness of wit, poorness in outward state, baseness of birth, etc. "For who makes you to differ from another?" 1 Cor. 4:7; either in natural gifts, as loveliness of body, beauty, feature, stature, wit, strength, etc.; see Job 10:10, 11; Ps. 139:13-15; in civil endowments, or any artificial skill, until it comes even unto matters of husbandry; see Isa. 28:24-28; in outward things; see Ps. 132; more particularly in preferment and promotion, see Ps. 75:6, 7; in children, 1 Sam. 1:27; Psalm 127:3; in a good wife; see Prov. 19:14; in spiritual things; see Ezek. 16; in anything you can name. We are all framed of the same mold, hewed out of the same rock, made as it were of the same cloth—the path of the scissors making the only difference between one person an another. It is therefore only the free love and grace of God which make all the difference. Whereupon it was an excellent speech of a French king, as his chronicler reports—"When I was born, there were a thousand other souls more born; what have I done unto God more than they? It is his mere grace and mercy which does often bind me more unto his justice; for the faults of great men are never small."

Let none then, I say, overlook, disdain, or brow-beat their brethren, by reason of any extraordinary gifts, eminence of parts, singularity of God's special favor, or indulgence towards him in any good thing, which he denies to others. Especially, yourself being vouchsafed the mercy of conversion, never insolently and imperiously demean those poor souls who are beside themselves in matters of salvation, who, like miserable drudges, damn themselves in the devil's slavery, and allow their corrupt nature to carry them to any villainy, lust, or lewd course. Alas! our hearts should bleed within us at beholding so many about us imbruing their cruel hands in the blood of their own souls, by their ignorance, worldliness, drunkenness, lust, lying, scoffing at piety, hating to be reformed, etc. What heart, except it be hewed out of the hard-est rock, or has sucked the breasts of merciless tigers—but would yearn and weep to see a man made of the same mold with him-self willfully, as it were, against the ministry of the word, a thou-sand warnings, and God's many compassionate invitations, cast himself, body and soul, into the endless, easeless, and remediless miseries of hell? And the rather should we pity and pray for such a one who follows the swing of his own heart to his own everlast-ing perdition, because the matter whereof we were all made is so nearly alike; only the free mercy, goodness, and grace of God make the difference. If God should give us over to the unbridled current of our corrupt nature we might be as bad, and run riot into a world of wickedness as well as he—if the same God visit him in mercy, he may become every way as good, or better than we.

3. If the free love of God be the fountain of all our good, away then with that feigned 'foresight of faith', right use of free will, and good works, which should move God to elect before all eternity; and that luciferian self-conceit of present merit, a fit monstrous brood of that beast of Rome, "who opposes and exalts himself above all that is called God," 2 Thess. 2:4. For 'foreseen meritorious works' are equally opposite to grace—as works meritorious really exist-ing. Here you must call to mind those eight considerations which I opposed against that wicked tenet of merit, which does justly deserve never to taste of God's free mercy.

II. Personal Goodness Brings Comfortable Blessings

The renown and honor of Noah's name; in that he stands here as the father of the new world, and the holy seed and progenitor of Jesus Christ. "These are the generations of Noah." Whereas the fame and memorial of all the families upon earth besides lay bur-ied and rotting in the gulf of everlasting oblivion, as their bodies in the universal grave of waters; the family of Noah, a righteous and holy man, is not only preserved in safety from the general deluge—but his generations registered and renowned in the book of God, and conveyed along towards the Lord Jesus, as his progenitors and precedent royal line.

Doctrine. Personal goodness is a good means to bring safety, honor, and many comfortable blessings upon posterity; see Deut. 5:29; Exod. 20:6; Ps. 37:25, 112:1-3; Prov. 20:1; 11:21; Acts 2:39.

REASONS

1. Parents professing true religion make conscience of pray-ing for their children before they have them, as did Isaac and Hannah; when their children were still in the womb. When they are born, as did Zacharias. In the whole course of their lives, as did Job. At their own death, as did Isaac—Gen. 25:21; 1 Sam. 1:10; Gen. 25:22; Luke 1:64; Job 1:5; Gen. 27:4. And prayers, we know, are, for the procuring of all favor at the hands of God, either for ourselves or others, the most undoubted sovereign means we can possibly use.

2. Godly parents do infinitely more desire to see the true fear of God planted in their children's hearts, than, if it were possible, the imperial diadem of the whole earth set upon their heads. And therefore their principal care is, and the crown of their greatest joy would be, by godly example, pious education, daily instruction, loving admonitions, seasonable reproofs, restraint from wicked company, the corruptions of the times, etc., by all dearest means and utmost endeavors, to leave them gracious when they die, and go out of this world. And "godliness," says Paul, "has the promise of the life that now is, and of that which is to come," 1 Tim. 4:8. It gives right and full interest to all the true honor, blessings, and comforts, which are to be had in heaven or in earth.

3. Children are ordinarily apt, out of a kindly instinct of natural lovingness, from many and strongest motives, to imitate and follow their parents either in baseness or godly demeanor, to heaven or hell.

4. A father who truly fears God dares not to heap up riches or purchase high stations for his children by wrong doing, or any wicked ways of getting; whereupon both he and his family fare far the better, and happily avoid the flaming edge of those many fearful curses denounced in God's book against all unjust dealers. Such as that, Eccles. 5:13, 14, "There is a sore evil *which* I have seen under the sun, namely, riches kept for their owners to their hurt. But those riches perish by evil use. And he brings forth a son, and nothing *is* in his hand." And Hab. 2:9, 10, "You are doomed! You have made your family rich with what you took by violence, and have tried to make your own home safe from harm and danger! But your schemes have brought shame on your family; by destroying many nations you have only brought ruin on yourself."

Use. 1. Would you, then, have your little babes you love so dearly, blessed upon earth, truly noble, God's favorites, and meet you in heaven? The be holy yourself! Men are very careful and curious to have their seed-corn and breed of cattle choice and generous; and will they not endeavor to nurture, manage, and conduct the immortal souls of their children with grace, by godly education, to the highest advancement of which those noble natures are capable, to everlasting bliss, fruition of all heavenly joys, and world without end?

2. This may also serve to reprove and correct those covetous madmen that labor more to have their children great than good, rich than religious. It is a madness of that kind which lacks terms to express it—that a man should go to hell himself, and fit his children to follow him, in seeking to establish his house and raise his posterity by sacrilege, simony, bribery, usury, oppression—or any other course of cruelty and wrong. For so they lay their foundation in fire-works, which is able to blow up themselves and their posterity, body and soul, root and branch!

3. Let this fill the heart of the dying Christian with sweetest peace. For, whereas the bloody knife of profane men's unconscionable and cruel negligence in training up their children religiously, does stick full deep in their souls, and, leaving this life, they bequeath unto them the curse of God, together with their ill-gotten goods. But the Christian happily finds his conscience, by reason of his former thirsty desire and sincere endeavor to do his children good spiritually, freed from the horror of such blood-guiltiness, and leaves them to that comfortable outward estate which no injury or usury has impoisoned, and to that never-failing providence of our heavenly Father, which then is accustomed to work most graciously and bountifully for us, when we, renouncing the arm of flesh, the favor of man, riches of iniquity, and all such broken reeds, depend most upon it. If we must needs be our own carvers for things of this life, either by right or wrong, fraud or fair dealing—so that we may thrive and grow great in the world—then we are justly cast off from all merciful care over us, and exposed to ruin and curse. But, if we rest sincerely for ourselves and our family upon the all-powerful Providence, it will never fail nor forsake us—but ever exercise and improve its sweetness and wisdom for our true and everlasting good.

III. In the third point, **we have a description of Noah's spiritual state, which is the complete character of a true Christian, consisting of three attributes—**

1. **Justness**.
2. **Sincerity**.
3. **Piety**.

I gather from the first attribute—Every truly religious man is also a righteous and true-dealing man.

I gather from the second attribute—Sincerity is the sinew and touchstone of true Christianity.

But these two I have so often pressed in the course of my ministry, that I will pass by them at this time.

See what kind of honesty to men that is, which is not accompanied with piety towards God; the same is that piety towards God which is not attended with honesty to men. Dishonest religion, irreligious honesty, insincere religion and honesty, are all of the same nature—and all out of the right path. If you have respect only to the commandments of the first table, and outward performance of religious services—but neglect duties of the second, and conscientious interactions with your brethren, you are but a pharisee and formal professor. If you deal justly with your neighbor—and yet are a stranger to the mystery of godliness, cannot pray, nor submit to a sincere and searching ministry, which the first table enjoins, you are but a mere moral man. If you put on a flourish and outward face only of obedience and conformity to both, and yet be true-hearted in neither, as did the pharisees, Matt. 23:14-23, you are but a gross hypocrite. Bear yourself **holy** towards God, **honestly** towards man, and trueheartedly towards both, or you are nothing in Christ's kingdom—but still in the gall of bitterness and bond of iniquity. Put on righteousness and true holiness in this life, Eph. 4:24, or you shall never put on a crown of glory in the life to come.

"In his generations," which were many, and mainly corrupt, Noah stood out, and stuck unto God through so many ages, and against so wicked a world; from which we may learn- Doctrine. That **consistency is ever an inseparable attendant upon true Christianity**. But because a double constancy is here implied,

1. One in respect of continuance of time.

2. Another in respect of opposition to the corruptions of the times.

I may observe two points.

1. Grace once truly rooted in the heart can never be removed. See for this purpose, Matt. 24:24; 1 John 2:19, 21; John 10:28; Rom. 8:35, 38, 39; Luke 22:32; 2 Cor. 1:21, 22; Eph. 4:30, etc. Proofs for this, may be taken from,

1. The dearness, strength, constancy, inviolableness of God the Father's love unto his children. It is dearer than a mother's to her sweetest babe, Isa. 49:15; it is stronger than the mountains, Isa. 54:10; it is as constant as the courses of the sun and moon and stars; of the day and of the night, Jer. 31:35, 36, and 33:20, 21; it is as sure as God himself, Ps. 89:33-35.

2. Christ's triumphant sitting down and intercession at his

Father's right hand; which may forever, with sweetest peace, and freedom from slavish trembling, assure us of our rootedness in Christ, constancy in grace, and everlasting abode with him in the other world. Being once implanted into Christ by a lively fruitful faith, and blessedly knit unto him by his Spirit, as fast as the sinews of his precious body are knit unto his bones, his flesh to his sinews, and his skin to his flesh—he that would tear us from Christ's mystical body, must pull him out of heaven, and remove him from the right hand of his Father. What furious or infernal power can or dare lay a finger on us in this kind? Christ has taken the poisoning power out of everything that would hurt us, or would drag us to hell. He has conquered, led captive, carried in triumph, and chained up forever, all the enemies of our souls, and enviers of our salvation. They may, in the meantime, exercise us for our good—but they shall never be able to execute their malicious wills, or mortally hurt us, either here, or in the next life.

3. The irrevocable sealing of the blessed Spirit, Eph. 1:13, 14, and. 4:30. And who or what can or dare reverse the deed, or break up the seal of the Holy Spirit? Here then, as you see, the blessed Trinity is the immovable ground of our continuing on in grace.

4. The lasting and immortal power of the word when once rooted in a good and honest heart, Luke 8:15; 1 Pet. 1:23.

5. The certainty and sweetness of **promises** to this purpose, Jer. 32:39, 40; Zech. 10:12; John 8:12; 2 Sam. 7:14, 15; Ps. 89:83-37.

6. The force and might of faith, 1 Pet. 1:2-9.

7. The efficacy of Christ's prayer, Luke 22:32; John 17:15-20; Rom. 8:34.

8. The durable vigor of saving graces, John 4:14; Rom. 11:29.

9. The inability, nay, impossibility, of all causes or creatures to pluck out of God's hand, John 10:29, or to draw any of his redeemed children to a total or final falling away. It is not the devil himself can do it, 1 John 5:18. It is not the world, 1 John 5:4; John 16:33. It is not the concurrent fury and united forces of all the powers of darkness, Matt. 16:18. It is not sin, 2 Sam. 7:14, 15; Ps. 89:81, 32. It is not weakness of faith, or other graces, Matt. 12:20. It is not the imposture of false prophets, Matt. 24:24. It is no creature, or created power, Rom. 8:38, 39.

USE

1. This point, thus confirmed, does confound that forlorn tenet of the popish teachers, which tells us that a justified and sanctified man may fall finally and totally from grace. In which I have heretofore upon another occasion, in your hearing, punctually re-

futed those which I conceived Bellarmine's best arguments. I will not now trouble you with his sophistry again.

2. This sweet and precious truth may crown the hearts of all those who are truly Christ's with unspeakable and glorious joy. Let new converts and babes in Christ, who are accustomed to be very fearful and much troubled lest they should not hold out, because upon their first entrance into the ways of christianity they are cunningly and concurrently encountered with so many oppositions—from the devil, who then rages extraordinarily; from the world, which then offers more and more alluring baits; from the flesh, which naturally is very impatient of any spiritual restraint; from carnal friends, who cannot endure their change; from their old companions, who cry out, 'they are turning puritans'; from the times, which discourage and look sourly upon their zeal; sometimes from the father who begat them; from the mother who nursed them; from the wife who lies in their bosom; from a world of enemies to grace.

I say, in such a case, let them grasp in the arms of their faith the proofs and promises in the present point, and ride on, because of the word of truth. Let them sweetly, with full assurance and unconquerable resolution, repose upon that everlasting encouragement, for the finishing of their spiritual building, which Zerubbabel received from the mouth of God himself, for success of the material building, a type of this—"Not by might nor by power—but by my Spirit, says the Lord Almighty. Who are you, O great mountain? before Zerubbabel you shall become a plain; and he shall bring forth the head stone thereof with shoutings, crying, Grace, grace unto it," Zech. 4:6, 7.

And that they may more comfortably and constantly go on, let them often cast their eyes upon these and the like cautions, at their very first giving their names unto Christ.

(1) Propose such **interrogations** as these to your own heart— Are you content to abandon your bosom sin, and the sensual froth of former pleasures, hereafter to delight in God, as your chief joy? Can you take up your cross, and follow Christ, his truth and holy ways, amidst the many by-paths that lead to hell, and different opinions of multitudes of men? Are you willing to suffer adversity, disgrace, and ridicule—with the righteous and despised godly ones? Can you endure to have things laid unto your charge, which you never did, thought, or dreamed of; to become the drunkard's song; a by-word to those that are viler than the earth; to be the song of ridicule at their feasts? Lam. 3:63. In a word—can you,

for Christ's sake, deny yourself, your worldly wisdom, natural wit, carnal friends, old companions, pleasures, profits, preferments, ease, excellency of learning, acceptance with the world, outward state, liberty, life, or whatever else you can name dearest unto flesh and blood? If your heart answers not affirmatively, (I mean, out of the resolution of a well-advised regenerate judgment; for I know the flesh will grumble and reclaim,) you will certainly fall away, or end in formality.

(2) Look to your **repentance**—that it be sincere, universal, constant, from the heart, for all known sins—to your dying day. 1. If some worldly cross be the continued principal motive of your repentance —2. or the humor of melancholy —3. if it be confusedly only for sin, and in general—4. or for someone special notorious sin only —5. or for some lesser sins, with neglect of greater, as for tithing mint, etc.—6. if it be only legal—7. but for some sins, of what kind soever; leaving but so much as one known sin not taken to heart—8. or but for a time—all will come to naught. A foundation of godly sorrow, deliberately, advisedly, and sincerely laid at first, will be forever after a comfortable encouragement to faith, spiritual joy, well-doing, and walking with God.

(3) Take the touchstone of fruitful, powerful, and special marks, to discern and distinguish justifying saving faith from all false and insufficient faiths; for a temporary faith may go far.

(4) Let knowledge and love grow up together in you, and mutually transfuse spiritual vigor into each other. Presume not upon any knowledge, without a humble inflamed love. Neither build too much upon the heat of zeal, without the light of knowledge—either of these may be single and superior in some, who afterwards may shamefully fall away.

(5) Above all things, look unto your heart. If your outward reformation were angelical, in words, actions, and all external demeanor—and yet your heart remained unchanged, you are but a painted tomb, and cannot be saved. Let a man take a wolf, beat it black and blue, break its bones, knock out its teeth, cut away its claws, put upon it a sheep's skin—yet still it retains its wolfish nature. In like manner, let a man become ever so harmless outwardly, yet without a new heart all is in vain.

(6) Incorporate yourself into the company of God's people, by all engagements and obligations of a profitable, intimate, and comfortable fellowship in the gospel. There is a secret tie unto perseverance, in the communion of saints. He is not likely to walk long that walks alone, especially if he might enjoy good company.

Shunning society with the godly, is a plain sign of a temporary faith.

(7) Consider well (for the contrary is a notable discovery of counterfeits) that your calling to grace must settle you more surely in your honest particular employment; and make you therein more faithful, conscientious, and laborious.

Let Christians also of longer standing, and more strength in their assaults on perseverance, have recourse unto this tower of truth, and labor to prevent that which they fear.

1. By constancy, in a careful use of all the means; the word, prayer, conference, meditation, sacraments, etc. To which, let them preserve their love, and practice what they hear, without omission or delay. He who gives way to a heartless neglect, or customary hardness of heart, in the use of the ordinances, may justly suspect his nearness to some fearful sin, or fierce temptation, to some heavy judgment, or dangerous apostasy.

2. As soon as they discover any spiritual weakness or decay, assault or temptation, let them often flee unto the throne of grace, and mightily oppose with the most fervent prayers of extraordinary private humiliation.

3. Let them keep perfection single in their eye and aim; and, towards the attainment thereof, acquire and acquaint themselves with rules of holy life, daily directions, and ways of the most godly and self-denying men.

4. Let them watchfully deny all occasions of falling back—spiritual pride, known hypocrisy, desire to be rich, undervaluing and declining the most searching means, negligence in pious duties, discontinuance of intimateness with the godly, etc.

5. Let them consider that all which is past is lost, if they fall off, 2 John 8.

This former point of constancy in grace did arise from a consideration of blessed Noah's continuance in goodness through so many ages. Now, in that he did not conform to the iniquities of the times—but did stand unstained, amidst the most wicked generations which ever dwelt upon earth, I gather the necessity of another constancy, and that is in respect of opposition to the corruptions of times.

SEVEN HINDRANCES WHICH KEEP BACK A SINNER FROM THE PRACTICE OF PIETY

I. The First Hindrance of Piety.

An ignorant mistaking of the true meaning of certain places of the holy Scriptures, and some other chief grounds of Christian religion.

The Scriptures mistaken are these:

1. Ezek 33:14, 16, "At what time soever a sinner repents of his sin, I will blot out all," etc. Hence the carnal professor gathers, that he may repent when he will. It is true, whensoever a sinner does repent, God will forgive; but the text says not, that a sinner may repent whensoever he will, but when God will give him grace. Many, when they would have repented, were rejected, and could not repent, though they sought it carefully with tears (Heb 12:17; Luke 13:24,27) What comfort yields this text to you who have not repented, nor know whether you shall have grace to repent hereafter?

2. Matt 11:28, "Come unto me, all you that labor and are heavy laden, and I will give you rest." Hence the lewdest man collects, that he may come unto Christ when he wills; but he must know that no man ever comes to Christ, but he who, as Peter says, having known the way of righteousness, has escaped the pollutions of the world, through the knowledge of our Lord and Savior Jesus Christ (2 Pet 2:20,22) To come unto Christ is to repent and believe (Isa 1:18; John 6:35) and this no man can do, except his heavenly Father draws him by his grace (John 6:4)

3. Rom 8:1, "There is therefore no condemnation to those who are in Christ Jesus." True; but they are such who walk not after the flesh, as you do, but after the Spirit, which you did never yet resolve to do.

4. 1 Tim 1:15, "Christ Jesus came into the world to save sinners," etc. True; but such sinners, who like Paul, are converted from their wicked life; not like you, who still continue in your lewdness: "For that grace of God which brings salvation unto all men, teaches us, that, denying ungodliness and worldly lusts, we should live soberly, righteously, and godly, in this present world." (Titus 2:11-12)

5. Prov 24:16, "A just man falls seven times in a day, and rises," etc. [in a day is not in the text:] which means not falling into sin, but falling into trouble, which his malicious enemy plots against the just, and from which God delivers him (Psalm 34:19) And though it meant falling in and rising out of sin, what is this to you, whose falls all men may see every day but neither God nor man can at any time see your rising again by repentance.

6. Isa 64:6, "All our righteousnesses are as filthy rags." Hence the carnal professor gathers, that, seeing the best works of the best saints are no better, then his are good enough; and therefore he needs not much grieve that his devotions are so imperfect. But Isaiah means not in this place the righteous works of the regenerate, as fervent prayers in the name of God; charitable alms from the affections of mercy; suffering in the gospel's defense, the confiscation of goods, and spilling of blood, and such works which Paul calls the fruit of the Spirit (Gal 5:22;) but the prophet, making a humble confession in the name of the Jewish church, when she had fallen from God to idolatry, acknowledges, that while they were by their filthy sins separated from God, as lepers are from men by their infecting sores and polluted clothes, their chief righteousness could not be but abominable in his sight. And though our best works, compared with Christ's righteousness, are no better than unclean rags; yet, in God's acceptance for Christ's sake, they are called white raiment (Rev 3:18), yes, pure fine linen and shining (Rev 19:8), far unlike the leopard's spots (Jer 13:23) and filthy garments (Zech 3:4)

7. James 3:2, "In many things we sin all" True; but God's children sin not in all things as you do, without either bridling their lusts or mortifying their corruptions. And though the relics of sin remain in the dearest children of God, that they had need daily to cry, "Our Father who is in heaven, forgive us our trespasses;" yet, in the New Testament, none are properly called sinners, but the unregenerate (Gal 1:15; Rom 5:8; John 9:31;) but the regenerate, in respect of their zealous endeavor to serve God in unfeigned holiness, are everywhere called saints; insomuch that John says, "Whoever is born of God sins not," (1 John 3:9; 1 John 5:18;) that is, lives not in willful filthiness, allowing sin to reign in him, as you do. Deceive not yourself with the name of a Christian; whoever lives in any customary gross sin, he lives not in the state of grace. "Let, therefore," says Paul, "everyone that names the name of Christ depart from iniquity:" (2 Tim 2:19) The regenerate sin, but upon frailty; they repent, and God does pardon; there they

sin not to death (1 John 5:16) The reprobate sin maliciously, sin-fully, and delight therein; so that by their good will, sin shall leave them before they will leave it; they will not repent, and God will not pardon; therefore their sins are mortal, says John, or rather immortal, as says Paul (Rom 2:5) It is no excuse, therefore, to say, we are all sinners: true Christians, you see, are all saints.

8. Luke 23:43. The thief converted at the last gasp, was received to paradise. What then? if I may have but time to say, when I am dying, "Lord have mercy upon me," I shall likewise be saved. But what if you shall not? and yet many in that day shall say, Lord, Lord, and the Lord will not know them (Matt 7:22-23) The thief was saved, for he repented; but his fellow thieve had no grace to repent, and was damned. Beware, therefore, lest, trusting to late repentance at your last end on earth, you be not driven to repent too late without end in hell.

9. 1 John 1:7, "The blood of Jesus Christ cleanses us from all sin." And 1 John 2:1, "If any man sins, we have an advocate with the Father, Jesus Christ the righteous," etc. O comfortable! but hear what John says in the same place, "My little children, these things write I unto you, that you sin not;" if, therefore, you leave your sin, these comforts are thine—else they belong not to you.

10. Rom 5:20, "Where sin abounded, grace did abound much more." O sweet! but hear what Paul adds, "What shall we say then? shall we continue in sin, that grace may abound? God forbid. How shall we that are dead to sin, live any longer therein?" (Rom 6:1-2) This place teaches us not to presume, but that we should not despair. None, therefore, of these promises, promises any grace to any but to the penitent heart.

The grounds of religion mistaken are these:

1. From the doctrine of **justification by faith alone**, a carnal professor gathers, that good works are not necessary. He commends others that do good works, but he persuades himself that he shall be saved by his faith, without doing any such matter. But he should know, that though good works are not necessary to justification, yet they are necessary to salvation: "For we are God's workmanship, created in Christ Jesus unto good works, which God has predestinated that we should walk in them." (Eph 2:10) Whoever, therefore, in years of discretion, brings not forth good works after he is called, he cannot be saved; neither was he ever predestinated to life eternal. Therefore the Scripture says, that Christ will reward every man according to his works (Rom 2:6; 2 Cor 9:6; Rev 22:12) Christ respects in the angels of the seven

churches nothing but their works (Rev 2:2;) and at the last day he will give the heavenly inheritance only to them who have done good works—in feeding the hungry, clothing the naked, etc. At that day righteousness shall wear the crown (Matt 25; 2 Tim 4:8) No righteousness, no crown—no good works, according to a man's talent, no reward from God, unless it be vengeance (Rom 2:8) To be rich in good works, is the surest foundation of our assurance to obtain eternal life (1 Tim 6:19;) for good works are the true fruits of a true faith, which apprehends Christ, and his obedience unto salvation. And no other faith in Christ avails, but that which works by love (Gal 5:6;) and (but in the act of justification) that faith which alone justifies, is never alone, but ever accompanied with good works: as the tree with his fruits, the sun with his light, the fire with his heat, and water with his moisture. And the faith which does not justify herself by good works before men, is but dead faith, which will never justify a man's soul before God (James 2:26) But a justifying faith purifies the heart and sanctifies the whole man throughout (Acts 15:9; Acts 16:18; 1 Thess 5:23)

2. From the doctrine of God's **eternal predestination** (Matt 25:24; Eph 1:4; Eccles 3:14) and unchangeable decree, he gathers, that if he be predestinated to be saved, he cannot but be saved; if to be damned, no means can do any good; therefore all works of piety are but in vain. But he should learn, that God has predestinated to the means, as well as to the end. Whom, therefore, God has predestinated to be saved, which is the end (1 Pet 1:9), he has likewise predestinated to be first called, justified, and made conformable to the image of his Son, which is the means (Rom 8:29-30; John 15:16) And they, says Peter, who are elect unto salvation, are also elect unto the sanctification of the spirit (1 Pet 1:2) If, therefore, upon your calling, you conform yourself to the word and example of Christ your master, and obey the good motions of the Holy Spirit, in leaving sin, and living a godly life, then assure yourself, that you are one of those who are infallibly predestinated to everlasting salvation. If otherwise, blame not God's predestination, but your own sin and rebellion. Do you but return to God, and God will graciously receive you, as the father did the prodigal son, and by your conversion, it shall appear both to angels and men, that you did belong to his election (Luke 15:10,24) If you will not, why should God save you?

3. When a carnal professor hears that **man has not freewill unto good**, he looses the reins to his own corrupt will, as though it lay not in him to bridle, or to subdue it: implicitly making God the

author of sin, in allowing man to run into this necessity. But he should know that God gave Adam freewill, to stand in his integrity if he would; but man, abusing his freewill, lost both himself and it. Since the fall, man in his state of corruption has freewill to evil, but not to good; for in this state, we are not, says the apostle, sufficient to think a good thought (2 Cor 3:5) And God is not bound to restore us what we lost so wretchedly, and take no more care to recover again. But as soon as a man is regenerated, the grace of God frees his will unto good; so that he does all the good things he does with a freewill: for so the apostle says, that God of his own good pleasure, works both the will and the deed in us, who, as the apostle expounds, cleanse ourselves from all filthiness of the flesh and spirit, and finish our sanctification in the fear of God (Phil 2:12-13; 2 Cor 7:1) And in this state, every true Christian has freewill, and as he increases in grace, so does his will in freedom: "For when the Son shall make us free, then shall we be free indeed," (John 8:36;) and where the Spirit of the Lord is, there is liberty (2 Cor 3:17;) for the Holy Spirit draws their minds, not by compulsion, but by the cords of love (Song 1:4), by illuminating their minds to know the truth; by changing their hearts to love the known truth; and by enabling every one of them (according to the measure of grace which he has received) to do the good which he loves. But you will not use the freedom of your will, so far as God has freed it; for you do many times willfully against God's law, to the hazard of your soul, which, if the king's law forbade under the penalty of death, or loss of your worldly estate, you would not do. Make not, therefore, your lack of freewill to good, to be so much the cause of your sin, as your lack of a loving heart to serve your heavenly Father.

4. When the natural man hears that no man, since the fall, is able to **fulfill the law of God**, and to keep all his commandments, he boldly presumes to sin as others do; he contents himself with a few good thoughts: and if he be not altogether as bad as the worst, he concludes that he is as truly regenerate as the best. And every voluntary refusal of doing good, or withstanding evil, he counts the impossibility of the law. But he should learn, that though, since the fall, no man but Christ, who was both God and man, did, or can perfectly fulfill the whole law, yet every true Christian, as soon as he is regenerate, begins to keep all God's commandments in truth, though he cannot in absolute perfection. Thus, with David, they apply their hearts to fulfill God's commandments always unto the end (Psalm 119:112) And then the Spirit of grace, which

was promised to be more abundantly poured forth under the gospel, helps them in their good endeavors, and assists them to do what he commands them to do (Joel 2:28-29; Zech 12:10) And in so doing, God accepts their good will and endeavor (2 Cor 8:12), Christ having fulfilled the law for us. And in this respect John says, that God's commandments are not burdensome (1 John 5:3) And Paul says, "I am able to do all things, through the help of him who strengthens me." (Phil 4:13) And Zacharias and Elizabeth are said to walk in all the commandments of the Lord without reproof (Luke 1:6) Hereupon Christ commends to his disciples the care of keeping his commandments, as the truest testimony of our love unto him (John 15:10)

So far, therefore, does a man love Christ, as he makes conscience to walk in his commandments; and the more unto Christ is our love, the less will our pains seem in keeping his law. The law's curse, which, under the Old Testament, was so terrible, is, under the New, by the death of Christ, abolished to the regenerate. The rigor which made it so impossible to our nature before, is now to the newborn so mollified by the Spirit, that it seems facile and easy. The apostles, indeed, pressed on the unconverted Jews and Gentiles the impossibility of keeping the law by ability of nature corrupted; but when they have to do with regenerate Christians, they require to the law, which is the rule of righteousness, true obedience in word and deed; the mortifying of their members; the crucifying of the flesh, with the affections and lusts thereof; resurrection to newness of life; walking in the Spirit; overcoming of the world by faith (Rom 15:18; Col 3:5; Gal 5:24-25; Rom 6:4-5,12-13; Rom 8:11; 1 John 5:4) So that, though no man can say as Christ, Which of you can rebuke me of sin? (John 8:46), yet every regenerate Christian can say of himself, Which of you can rebuke me of being an adulterer, whoremonger, swearer, drunkard, thief, usurer, oppressor, proud, malicious, covetous, profaner of the Sabbath, a liar, a neglector of God's public service, and such like gross sins? else he is no true Christian. When a man casts off the conscience of being ruled by God's law, then God gives him over to be led by his own lusts, the surest sign of a reprobate sense (Rom 1:24,28) Thus the law, which, since the fall, no man by his own natural ability can fulfill, is fulfilled in truth of every regenerate Christian, through the gracious assistance of Christ's Holy Spirit (Rom 8:9, etc) And this Spirit God will give to every Christian that will pray for it, and will incline his heart to keep his laws (Luke 11:13; James 1:5)

5. When the unregenerate man hears that **God delights more in the inward mind than in the outward man**, then he imagines that all outward reverence and profession is but either superstitious or superfluous. Hence it is that he seldom kneels in the church; that he puts on his hat at singing of psalms, and the public prayers; which the profane varlet would not offer to do in the presence of a prince or a nobleman. And so that he keep his mind unto God, he thinks he may fashion himself, in other things, to the world. He divides his thoughts, and gives so much to God, and so much to his own lusts; yes, he will divide with God the Sabbath, and will give him almost the one half, and spend the other wholly in his own pleasures. But know, O carnal man, that Almighty God will not be served by halves, because he has created and redeemed the whole man! And as God detests the service of the outward man, without the inward heart, as hypocrisy; so he counts the inward service, without all external reverence, to be mere profaneness: he requires both in his worship. In prayer, therefore, bow your knees, in witness of your humiliation; lift up your eyes and your hands, in testimony of your confidence; hang down your head and smite your bosom, in token of your contrition; but especially call upon God with a sincere heart—serve him holily, serve him wholly, serve him only; for God and the Prince of this world are two contrary masters, and therefore no man can possibly serve both.

6. The unregenerate professor holds the hearing of the gospel preached, to be but an indifferent matter, which he may use, or not use, at his pleasure. But whoever you are, that will be assured in your heart that you are one of Christ's elect sheep, you must have a special care and conscience (if possibly you can) to hear God's word preached. For,

First, the preaching of the gospel is the chief ordinary means which God has appointed to convert the souls of all that he has predestinated to be saved (Acts 13:48:) therefore it is called "the power of God unto salvation to everyone that believes." (Rom 1:16) And where this divine ordinance is not, the people perish (Prov 29:18;) and whoever shall refuse it, "it shall be more tolerable for the land of Sodom and Gomorrah in the day of judgment than for these people." (Matt 10:22)

Secondly, the preaching of the gospel is the standard or ensign of Christ (Isa 11:1), to which all soldiers and elect people must assemble themselves: when this ensign is displayed, as upon the Lord's day, he is none of Christ's people that flocks not unto it (Isa

2:2;) neither shall any drop of the rain of his grace light on their souls (Zech 14:17)

Thirdly, it is the ordinary means by which the Holy Spirit begets faith in our hearts (Rom 10:14), without which we cannot please God (Heb 11:6) If the hearing of Christ's voice be the chief mark of Christ's elect sheep, and of the bridegroom's friend (John 10:27; John 3:29), then must it be a fearful mark of a reprobate goat (Heb 2; John 8:47) either to neglect or despise to hear the preaching of the gospel. Let no man think this position foolish, for "by this foolishness of preaching it pleases God to save those who believe." (1 Cor 1:11) Their state is therefore fearful who live in peace, without caring for the preaching of the gospel. Can men look for God's mercy, and despise his means? "He," says Christ of the preachers of his gospel, "that despises you, despises me." (Luke 10:16) "He who is of God hears God's words: you therefore hear them not, because you are not of God." (John 8:4,7) Had not the Israelites heard the message of Phinehas, they had never wept (Judg 2:1, etc) Had not the Baptist preached, the Jews had never mourned (Luke 7:32-33) Had not they who crucified Christ heard Peter's sermon, their hearts had never been pricked (Acts 2:37) Had not the Ninevites heard Jonah's preaching, they had never repented (Jon 3:5;)—and if you will not hear, and repent, you shall never be saved (Prov 28:9; Luke 13:5)

7. The opinion that **the sacraments** are but bare signs and seals of God's promise and grace to us, does not a little hinder piety: whereas, indeed, they are seals, as well of our service and obedience unto God; which service if we perform not to him, the sacraments seal no grace to us. But if we receive them, upon the resolution to be his faithful and penitent servants, then the sacraments do not only signify and offer, but also seal and exhibit indeed the inward spiritual grace which they outwardly promise and represent. And to this end baptism is called the "washing of regeneration, and renewing of the Holy Spirit," (Titus 3:5;) and the Lord's Supper, "the communion of the body and blood of Christ." (1 Cor 10:16) Were this truth believed, the holy sacrament of the Lord's Supper would be more often, and with greater reverence received.

8. The last, and not the least block at which piety stumbles in the course of religion, is by **adorning vices with the names of virtues**: as to call drunken carousing, drinking of healths; spilling innocent blood, valor; gluttony, hospitality; covetousness, thriftiness; whoredom, loving a mistress; simony, gratuity; pride, gracefulness; dissembling, compliment; children of Belial, good-

fellows; wrath, hastiness; ribaldry, mirth: so, on the other side, to call sobriety in words and actions, hypocrisy; alms-deeds, vainglory; devotion, superstition; zeal in religion, Puritanism; humility, crouching; scruple of conscience, preciseness, etc. And while thus we call evil good, and good evil, true piety is much hindered in her progress.

And thus much of the first hindrance of piety, by mistaking the true sense of some special places of Scripture, and grounds of Christian religion.

II. The Second Hindrance of Piety.

The evil example of great people, the practice of whose profane lives they prefer for their imitation before the precepts of God's holy word: so that, when they see the greatest men in the state, and many chief gentlemen in their country, to make neither care nor conscience to hear sermons, to receive the communion, nor to sanctify the Lord's Sabbaths, etc., but to be swearers, adulterers, carousers, oppressors, etc., then they think that the using of these holy ordinances are not matters of so great importance; for if they were, such great and wise men would not set so little value on them. Hereupon they think that religion is not a matter of necessity; and therefore, where they should, like **Christians, row against the stream of impiety towards heaven, they allow themselves to be carried with the multitude downright to hell, thinking it impossible that God will allow so many to be damned**: whereas, if the god of this world had not blinded the eyes of their minds, the holy Scriptures would teach them, that "not many wise men after the flesh, not many mighty, not many noble are called," etc. (1 Cor 1:26;) but that for the most part the poor receive the gospel, and that few rich men shall be saved (Matt 11:5; Matt 19:23-24;) and that howsoever many are called, yet the chosen are but few. Neither did the multitude ever save any from damnation (Matt 22:14)

As God has advanced men in greatness above others, so does God expect that they in religion and piety should go before others; otherwise greatness abused, in the time of their stewardship, shall turn to their greater condemnation in the day of their accounts. At what time sinful great and mighty men, as well as the poorest slaves and bondmen, shall wish that the rocks and mountains should fall upon them, and hide them from the presence of the Judge, and from his just deserved wrath (Rev 6:15-16, etc), it will prove but a miserable solace to have a great company of great men partakers with you of your eternal torments. The multitude of sinners does not extenuate, but aggravate sin, as in Sodom. Better it is, therefore, with a few to be saved in the ark, than, with the whole world, to be drowned in the flood. Walk with the few godly in the narrow path to heaven; but crowd not with the godless multitude in the broad way to hell (Exod 23:2) Let not the example of irreligious great men hinder your repentance; for their greatness cannot at that day exempt themselves from their own most grievous punishment.

III. The Third Hindrance of Piety.

The long escaping of deserved punishment in this life. "Because sentence," says Solomon, "is not speedily executed against an evil worker, therefore the hearts of the children of men are fully set in them to do evil, not knowing that the bountifulness of God leads them to repentance." (Eccles 8:11; Rom 2:4; 2 Pet 3:10) But when his patience is abused, and man's sins are ripened, his justice will at once both begin, and make an end of the sinner (1 Sam 3:12; Ezek 39:8;) and he will recompense the slowness of his delay with the grievousness of his punishment. Though they were allowed to run on the score all the days of their life, yet they shall be sure to pay the utmost farthing at the day of their death. And while they suppose themselves to be free from judgment, they are already smitten with the heaviest of God's judgments—a heart that cannot repent (Rom 2:5) The stone in the kidneys or gallbladder is a grievous pain that kills many a man's body; but there is no disease to the stone in the heart, whereof Nabal died, and which kills millions of souls (1 Sam 25:17) They refuse the trial of Christ and his cross; but they are stoned by hell's executioner to eternal death.

Because many nobles and gentlemen are not smitten with present judgment for their outrageous swearing, adultery, drunkenness, oppression, profaning of the Sabbath, and disgraceful neglect of God's worship and service, they begin to doubt of divine **providence** and **justice**—both which two eyes they would as willingly put out in God, as the Philistines bored out the eyes of Sampson. It is greatly therefore to be feared lest they will provoke the Lord to cry out against them, as Sampson against the Philistines (Judg 16:21) By neglecting the law, and walking after their own hearts, they put out, as much as in them lies, the eyes of my providence and justice; lead me therefore to these chief pillars (Judg 16:26, etc) whereupon the realm stands, that I may pull the realm upon their heads, and be at once avenged of them for my two eyes. Let not God's patience hinder your repentance; but because he is so patient, therefore do you the rather repent.

IV. The Fourth Hindrance of Piety.

Presumption on God's mercy. For when men are justly convinced of their sins, forthwith they betake themselves to this shield— Christ is merciful: so that every sinner makes Christ the patron of his sin: As though he had come into the world to bolster sin, and not to destroy the works of the devil (John 3:3) Hereupon the carnal professor presumes, that though he continues a while longer in his sin, God will not shorten his days. But what is this but to be an implicit atheist? Doubting that either God sees not his sins; or if he does, that he is not just: for if he believes that God is just, how can he think that God, who for sin so severely punishes others, can love him who still loves to continue in sin? True it is, Christ is merciful; but to whom? Only to those who repent and turn from iniquity in Jacob. (Isa 59:20) But if any man blesses himself in his heart, saying, 'I shall have peace, although I walk according to the stubbornness of mine own heart, thus adding drunkenness to thirst,' the Lord will not be merciful to him, etc. (Deut 29:19) O madmen! who dare bless themselves, when God pronounces them accursed! Look, therefore, how far you are from finding repentance in yourself; so far are you from any assurance of finding mercy in Christ. "Let, therefore, the wicked forsake his ways, and the unrighteous his own imaginations, and return unto the Lord, and he will have mercy upon him; and to our God, for he is very ready to forgive." (Isa 55:7)

Despair is nothing so dangerous as presumption; for we read not in all the Scriptures of above three or four whom roaring despair overthrew: but secure presumption has sent millions to perdition without any noise. As, therefore, the damsels of Israel sang in their dances, "Saul has killed his thousands and David his ten thousands," (1 Sam 18:7;) so may I say, that despair of God's mercy has damned thousands, but the presumption of God's mercy has damned ten thousands, and sent them quick to hell, where now they remain in eternal torments, without all help of ease, or hope of redemption. God spared the thief but not his fellow (Luke 18:43) **God spared one, that no man might despair: God spared but one, that no man should presume.** Joyful assurance to a sinner that repents: no comfort to him that remains impenitent. God is infinite in mercy, but only to those who turn from their sins, to serve him in holiness, "without which no man shall see the Lord." (Heb 12:14) To keep you, therefore, from presuming, remember that as Christ is a Savior, so Moses is an accuser (John 5:45) Live, therefore, as though there were no gospel: die as though there were no law. Pass your life as though you were under the conduct of Moses: depart this life as if you knew none but Christ, and him crucified. Presume not, if you will not perish: repent if you will be saved.

V. The Fifth Hindrance of Piety.

Evil company, commonly termed good-fellows—but indeed, the devil's chief instruments, to hinder a wretched sinner from repentance and piety. The first sign of God's favor to a sinner is, to give him grace to forsake evil companions: such who willfully continue in sin, despise the means of their calling, jeering at the sincerity of profession in others, and shaming the Christian religion by their own profane lives. These sit in the seat of the scorners (Psalm 1:1) For as soon as God admits a sinner to be one of his people, he bids him come out of Babylon (Rev 18:4) Every lewd company is a Babylon, out of which, let every child of God either keep himself; or if he be in, think that he hears his Father's voice sounding in his ear, "Come out of Babylon, my child." As soon as Christ looked in mercy upon Peter, he went out of the company that was in the high priest's hall, and wept bitterly for his offence (Luke 22:62) David vowing (upon recovery) a new life, said, "Away from me, all you workers of iniquity," etc. (Psalm 6:8), as if it were impossible to become a new man, until he had shaken off all old evil companions. The truest proof of a man's religion is the quality of his companions. Profane companions are the chief enemies of piety, and quellers of holy motions. Many a time is poor Christ (offering to be newborn in you) thrust into the stable, (Luke 2:7), when these lewd companions, by their drinking, plays, and jests, take up all the best rooms in the inn of your heart. O let not the company of earthly sinners hinder you from the society of heavenly saints and angels!

VI. The Sixth Hindrance of Piety.

A conceited fear, lest the practice of piety should make a man (especially a young man) to become too sad and pensive: whereas, indeed, none can better joy nor have more cause to rejoice, than pious Christians. For as soon as they are justified by faith they have peace with God (Rom 5:2), than which there can be no greater joy. Besides, they have already the kingdom of grace descended into their hearts, as an assurance that, in God's good time, they shall ascend into his kingdom of glory.

This **kingdom of grace** consists in three things—First, **Righteousness** (Rom 14:17;) for having Christ's righteousness to justify them before God, they endeavor to live righteously before men. Secondly, **Peace**; for the peace of conscience inseparably follows a righteous life. Thirdly, The **joy** of the Holy Spirit; which joy is only felt in the peace of a good conscience: and is so great, that it passes all understanding (Phil 4:7) No tongue can express it, no heart can conceive it, but only he who feels it. This is that fullness of joy which Christ promised his disciples in the midst of their troubles, a joy that no man could take from them (John 16:22) The feeling of this joy, David, upon his repentance, begged so earnestly at the hand of God—"Restore me to the joy of your salvation." (Psalm 51:12) And if the angels in heaven rejoice so much at the conversion of a sinner, the joy of a sinner converted must needs be exceeding great in his own heart (Luke 15:7,10) It is worldly sorrow that snows so heavily upon men's heads, and fills the furrows of their hearts with the sorrows of death (2 Cor 7:10)

The godly sorrow of the godly (when God thinks it fit to try them) causes in them repentance not to be repented of: for it does but further their salvation. And in all such tribulation, they shall be sure to have the Holy Spirit to be their comforter (John 14:16-17;) who will make our consolations to abound through Christ, as the sufferings of Christ shall abound in us (2 Cor 1:5) But while a man lives in impiety, he has no peace, says Isaiah (Isa 57:21) His laughter is but madness, says Solomon (Eccles 2:9;) his riches are but clay, says Habakkuk (Hab 2:6:) nay, the apostle esteems them no better than dung in comparison of the pious man's treasure (Phil 3:8; Luke 6:25;) all his joys shall end in woe, says Christ. Let not, therefore, this false fear hinder you from the practice of piety. **Better it is to go sickly with Lazarus to heaven; than full of mirth and pleasure, with the rich man to hell. Better it is to mourn for a time with men, than to be tormented forever with devils.**

VII. The Seventh Hindrance of Piety.

And lastly, the hope of long life: For, were it possible that a wicked liver thought this year to be his last year, this month his last month, this week his last week—he would change and amend his wicked life. He would use the best means to repent, and to become a new man. But as the rich man in the gospel promised himself many years to live in ease, mirth, and fullness (Luke 12:19-20), when he had not one night to live longer: so many wicked epicures falsely promise themselves the age of many years, when the thread of their life is already almost drawn out to an end. So Jeremiah ascribes the cause of the Jews' sins and calamities to this, that she remembered not her last end (Lam 1:9)

The longest space between a man's coming by the womb, and

going by the grave, is but short: for "man that is born of a woman has but a short time to live," (Job 14:1;) he has but a few days, and those full of nothing but troubles. And except the practice of piety, how much better is the state of the child that yesterday was born, and today is buried, than Methuselah's, who lived nine hundred sixty-nine years, and then died? Of the two, happier the babe, because he had less sin, and fewer sorrows. And what now remains of both, but a bare remembrance? What trust should a man repose in long life? seeing **the whole life of man is nothing but a lingering death**; so that, as the apostle protests, a man dies daily.

Harken, O secure fellow! your life is but a puff of breath in your nostrils; trust not to it (Isa 2:22) Your soul dwells in a house of clay, that will fall before it be long; as may appear by the dimness of your eyes, the deafness of your ears, the wrinkles in your cheeks, the rottenness of your teeth, the weakness of your sinews, the trembling of your hands, the brittleness in your bones, the shortness of your sleep, and every grey hair, as so many summoners, bid you prepare for your long home. Come, let us in the meanwhile walk to your father's coffin: break open the lid; see here, how that "corruption is your father, and the worm your mother and sister." (Job 17:14) See how these are? so must you be before long. Fool! you know not how soon. Your hourglass runs out rapidly, death in the meanwhile waits for you.

The whole life of man, save what is spent in God's service, is but foolery: for a man lives forty years before he knows himself to be a fool; and by that time he sees his folly, his life is finished.

Hark, farmer, before you see many more crops of harvest, yourself shall be ripe, and death will cut you down with his sickle. Hark, tradesman, before many months go over, your last month will come on; after which you will trade no longer. Hark, most grave judge, within a few terms, the term of your life approaches, wherein you shall cease to judge others, and go yourself to be judged. Hark, O man of God, that go to the pulpit, preach this sermon as it were the last that you should make to your people. Hark, nobleman, lay aside the high conceit of your honor: death, before it be long, will lay your honor in the dust, and make you as contemptible as the earth that you tread under your feet. Hark, you that now read this book, assure yourself, before it be long there will be but two holes where now your two eyes are placed; and others shall read the truth of this lesson upon your bare skull, which now you read in this little book. How soon I know not; but this I am sure of, that your time is appointed, your months are determined; your days are numbered, and your very last hour is limited (Job 14:5,14; Psalm 90:12; Dan 5:26; Dan 11:8), beyond which you shall not pass.

For then the messenger of death, mounted on his pale horse (Rev 6:8), shall alight at your door; and, notwithstanding all your wealth, your honor, and the tears of your dearest friends—will carry you away, bound hand and foot, as his prisoner, and keep your body under a load of earth, until that day comes wherein you must be brought forth to receive according to the things which you have done in that body, whether it be good or evil (2 Cor 5:10) O let not, then, the false hope of an uncertain long life hinder you from becoming a present practicer of piety! God offers grace for to-day; but who promises tomorrow? (Psalm 95:7; Heb 3:7, 13) There are now in hell many young men who had purposed to repent in their old age; but death cut them off in their impenitency, before ever they could attain to the time they set for their repentance. The longer a man runs in a disease, the harder it is to be cured: for *custom of sin* breeds hardness of heart, and the impediments which hinder you from repenting now, will hinder you more when you are more aged.

A wise man being to go a far and difficult journey, will not lay the heaviest burden upon the weakest horse. And with what conscience can you lay the great load of repentance on your feeble and tired old age? whereas now in your chief strength you cannot lift it, but are ready to stagger under it. Is it wisdom for him that is to sail a long and dangerous voyage, to lie playing and sleeping while the wind serves, and the sea is calm, the ship sound, the pilot well, mariners strong; and then set forth when the winds are contrary, the weather tempestuous, the sea raging, the ship rotten, the pilot sick, and the sailors languishing? Therefore, O sinful soul, begin now your conversion to God, while life, health, strength, and youth last: "before those years draw near, when you shall say. I have no pleasure in them." (Eccles 12:1)

God ever required in his service the firstborn, and the first fruits, and those to be offered to him without delay (Exod 13:2; Exod 22:29) So just Abel offered to God his firstlings and fattest lambs (Gen 4:4) and good reason that the best Lord should be first and best served. All God's servants should therefore remember to serve their Creator in the days of their youth (Eccles 12:12), and early in the morning, like Abraham, to sacrifice unto God the young Isaac of their old age (Gen 22:3) "You shall not see my face," says Joseph to his brethren, "except you bring your brother with you."

(Gen 43:3) And how shall you look in the face of Jesus, if you give your younger years to the devil, and bring him nothing but your blind, lame, and decrepit old age? "Offer it unto your prince," says Malachi. (Mal 1:8) If he will not accept such a one to serve him, how shall the Prince of princes admit such a one to be his servant? If the king of Babel would have young men (well-favored, and such as had ability in them) to stand in his palace, shall the King of heaven have none to stand in his courts but the blind and lame, such as the soul of David hated? (Dan 1:4; 2 Sam 5:8)

Do you think, when you have served Satan with your prime years, to satisfy God with your senility? Take heed lest God turn you over to your old master again; that as you have all the days of your life done his work, so he may in the end pay you your wages. Is that time fit to undertake, by the serious exercises of repentance (which is the work of works), to turn your sinful soul to God, when you are not able with all your strength to turn your weary bones on your soft bed? If you find it so hard a matter now, you shall find it far harder then. For your sin will wax stronger, your strength will grow weaker, your conscience will clog you, pain will distract you, the fear of death will amaze you, and the visitation of friends will so disturb you—that if you be not furnished aforehand with store of faith, patience, and consolation, you shall net be able either to meditate yourself, or to hear the word of comfort from others; nor to pray alone, nor to join with others who pray for you. It may be you shall be taken with a deadly senselessness, that you shall neither remember God, nor think upon your own state: and do you not well deserve that God should forget to save you in your death, who are so unmindful now to serve him in your life? The fear of death will drive many at that time to cry, Lord, Lord! but Christ protests that he will not then know them for his (Matt 7:22) Yes, many shall then, like Esau, with tears seek to repent, and yet then find no place of repentance (Heb 12:17) For man has not freewill to repent when he will—but only when God will give him grace.

And if **mercy** showed herself so inexorable, that she would not open her gates to so tender suitors as virgins, to so earnest suitors as knockers, because they knocked too late (Matt 25:11)—do you think that she will ever allow you to enter her gates, being so impure a wretch that never think to leave sin until sin first leaves you, and did never yet knock with your own fists upon the breasts of a penitent heart?

And justly does **grace** deny to open the gates of heaven, when you knock in your adversity, who in your prosperity would not allow Christ, while he knocked, to enter in at the door of your heart (Rev 3:20)—Trust not either late repentance or long life. Not late repentance; because it is much to be feared lest the repentance which the fear of death enforces, dies with a man dying; and the hypocrite, who deceived others in his life, may deceive himself in his death. God accepts none but freewill offerings, and the repentance that pleases him must be voluntary, and not of constraint. Not long life, for old age will fall upon the neck of youth: and **as nothing is more sure than death, so nothing is more uncertain than the time of dying**. Yes, often when ripeness of sin is hastened by outrageousness of sinning, God suddenly cuts off such wicked livers, either with the sword, intemperateness, luxury, surfeit, or some other fearful manner of sickness. May you not see that it is the evil spirit that persuades you to defer your repentance until old age, when experience tells you that not one of a thousand that takes your course ever attains to it? Let God's Holy Spirit move you not to give yourself any longer to eat and drink with the drunken, lest your Master sends death for you in a day when you look not for him, and in an hour that you are not aware of, and so suddenly cut you off, and appoint you your portion with the hypocrites, where shall be weeping and gnashing of teeth (Matt 27:49-51)

But if you love long life, fear God, and long for life everlasting (Deut 30:16; Prov 3:2; Psalm 34:11, etc) The longest life here, when it comes to the end, will appear to have been but as a tale that is told, a vanishing vapor, a flitting shadow, a seeming dream, a glorious flower, growing and flourishing in the morning, but in the evening cut down and withered (Psalm 90:9; James 4:14; Psalm 109:23; Psalm 76:5; Psalm 90:5-6; 1 Pet 1:24;) or like a weaver's shuttle, which, by winding here and there swiftly, unwinds itself to an end (Isa 38:12) It is but a moment, says Paul (2 Cor 4:17) **O the madness of man, that for a moment of sinful pleasure will hazard the loss of an eternal weight of glory!** (Heb 10:25; 2 Cor 4:17)

These are the seven chief hinderers of piety, which must be cast out, like Mary Magdalene's seven devils, before ever you can become a true practicer of piety, or have any sound hope to enjoy either favor from Christ by grace, or fellowship with him in glory (Mark 16:9; Luke 8:2)

The Conclusion

To conclude all. Forasmuch as you see that without Christ you are but a slave of sin, death's vassal, and the food of worms, whose thoughts are vain—whose deeds are vile—whose pleasures have scarcely a beginning—whose miseries never know end: what wise man would incur these hellish torments, though he might, by living in sin, purchase to himself for a time the empire of Augustus, the riches of Croesus, the pleasures of Solomon, the policy of Ahithophel, the voluptuous fare and fine apparel of the rich man? For what should it avail a man, as our Savior says, to win the whole world for a time, and then to lose his soul in hell forever?

And seeing that likewise you see how great is your happiness in Christ, and how vain are the hindrances that debar you from it; beware, as the apostle exhorts, of the deceitfulness of sin (Heb 3:13;) for **that sin, which seems now to be so pleasing to your corrupt nature, will one day prove the bitterest enemy to your distressed soul**, and in the meanwhile harden, unawares, your impenitent heart.

Sin, as a serpent, seems beautiful to the eye, but take heed of the sting behind, whose venomous effects, if you knew, you would as carefully fly from sin as from a serpent. For,

1. Sin did never any man good: and the more sin a man has committed, the more odious he has made himself to God, the more hateful to all godly men.

2. Sin brought upon you all the evil, crosses, losses, disgraces, and sicknesses, which ever befell you: "Fools;" says David, "by reason of their transgressions, and because of their iniquities, are afflicted." (Psalm 107:17) Jeremiah in a lamenting manner asks the question, "Why is the living man sorrowful?" (Lam 3:20) The Holy Spirit answers him, "Man suffers for his sin." Hereupon the prophet takes up that doleful outcry against sin, as the cause of all their miseries, "Woe now unto us that ever we have sinned!" (Lam 5:16)

3. If you do not speedily repent you of your sins, they will bring upon you yet far greater plagues, losses, crosses, shame, and judgments, than hitherto ever befell you. (Read Lev 26:18, etc.; Deut 28:15, etc)

4. And lastly, If you will not cast off your sin; God, when the measure of your iniquity is full, will cast you off for your sin (Gen 15:6;) for as he is just, so he has power to kill and cast into hell all hardened and impenitent sinners. If, therefore, you will avoid the cursed effects of sin in this life, and the eternal wrath due to it in the world to come, and be assured that you are not one of those who are given over to a reprobate mind; let then, O sinner, my counsel be acceptable unto you! break off your sins by righteousness. O let there at length be an healing of your error!

(Dan 4:27) Nathan used but one parable, and David was converted (Sam 12:13;) Jonah preached but once to Nineveh, and the whole city repented (Jonah 3:5, etc.;) Christ looked but once on Peter, and he went out and wept bitterly (Luke 22:62) And now that you are oft and so lovingly entreated, not by a prophet, but by Christ the Lord of prophets; yes, that God himself, by his ambassadors, begs you to be reconciled to him (2 Cor 5:20), leave off your adultery with David; repent of your sins like a true Ninevite; and while Christ looks in mercy upon you, leave your wicked companions, and weep bitterly for your offences.

Content not yourself with that formal religion which unregenerate men have framed to themselves, instead of sincere devotion; for in the multitude of opinions, most men have almost lost the practice of true religion. Think not that you are good enough, because you do as the most, and are not so bad as the worst. No man is so wicked that he is addicted to all kind of vices, for there is an antipathy between some vices; but remember that Christ says, "Except your righteousness shall exceed the righteousness of the scribes and Pharisees, you shall in no case enter into the kingdom of heaven." (Matt 5:20) Consider with yourself how far you come short of the Pharisees, in fasting, praying, frequenting the church, and giving of alms: think with yourself how many pagans who never knew baptism, yet in moral virtues and honesty of life, do go far beyond you—where is then the life of Christ your master? and how far are you from being a true Christian?

If you do willingly yield to live in any one gross sin, you cannot have a regenerate soul, though you reform yourself, like Herod, from many other vices. A true Christian must have respect to walk, in the truth of his heart, in **all** the commandments of God alike (Mark 6:20) "For," says James, "he who shall offend in one point of the law" (willfully) "is guilty of all." (James 2:10) And Peter bids us lay aside, not some, but "**all** malice, guile, and hypocrisies," etc. (1 Pet 2:1) One sin is enough to damn a man's soul, without repentance. Dream not to go to heaven by any nearer or easier way than Christ has trained unto us in his word: the way to heaven is not easy or common, but straight and narrow (Matt 7:14;) yes, so narrow, that Christ protests that a rich man shall hardly enter into the kingdom of heaven (Matt 19:23), and that those that enter are but a few (Matt 7:14; Matt 22:14), and that those few cannot get in but by striving (Luke 13:24), and that some of those who strive to enter in shall not be able. This all God's saints, while they lived here, knew well; when with so often fastings, so earnest prayers, so frequent hearing the word, and receiving the sacraments, and with such abundance of tears they devoutly begged at the hands of God, for Christ's sake, to be received into his kingdom.

If you will not believe this truth, I assure you that the devil, who persuades you now that it is easy to attain heaven, will tell you hereafter that it is the hardest business in the world. If, therefore, you are desirous to purchase sound assurance of salvation to your soul, and to go the right and safe way to heaven, get forthwith, like a wise virgin (Matt 25:1), the oil of piety in the lamp of your conversation, that you may be in a continual readiness to meet the bridegroom, whether he comes by death or by judgment.

HOW TO BEGIN THE MORNING WITH PIOUS MEDITATIONS AND PRAYER

As soon as ever you awake in the morning, keep the door of your heart fast shut, that no earthly thought may enter, before God comes in; and let him, before all others, have the first place there. So all evil thoughts either will not dare to come in, or shall the easier be kept out; and the heart will more savor of piety and godliness all the day after. But if your heart be not, at your first waking, filled with some meditations of God and his word, and dressed, like the lamp in the tabernacle (Exod 27:20-21), every morning and evening, with the oil-olive of God's word, and perfumed with the sweet incense of prayer (Exod 30:6-7), Satan will attempt to fill it with worldly cares or fleshly desires, so that it will grow unfit for the service of God all the day after, sending forth nothing but the stench of corrupt and lying words, and of rash and blasphemous thoughts.

Begin, therefore, every day's work with God's word and prayer; and offer up to God upon the altar of a contrite heart, the groans of your spirit, and the calves of your lips, as your morning sacrifice, and the first fruits of the day (Psalm 51:17; Rom 8:22; Hos 13:2; Psalm 130:6;) and as soon as you awake say to him thus:

My soul waits on you, O Lord, more than watchmen watch for the morning! O God, therefore be merciful unto me, and bless me, and cause your face to shine upon me! Fill me with your mercy this morning, so shall I rejoice and be glad all my days.

Meditations for the Morning.

1. The Almighty God can, in the resurrection, as easily raise up your body out of the grave, from the sleep of death, as he has this morning wakened you in your bed, out of the sleep of nature. At the dawning of which resurrection day, Christ shall come to be glorified in his saints; and every one of the bodies of the thousands of his saints, being fashioned like unto his glorious body, shall shine as bright as the sun (2 Thess 1:10; Jude 14; Phil 3:21; Luke 9:31;) all the angels shining likewise in their glory; the body of Christ surpassing them all in splendor and glory; and the Godhead excelling it. If the rising of one sun makes the morning sky so glorious, what a bright shining and glorious morning will that be,

when so many thousand thousands of bodies, far brighter than the sun, shall appear and accompany Christ as his glorious train, coming to keep his general session of righteousness, and to judge the wicked angels, and all ungodly men (Acts 17:31; 1 Cor 6:3; Jude 15;) and let not any transitory profit, pleasure, or vain glory of this day, cause you to lose your part and portion of the eternal bliss and glory of that day, which is properly termed the resurrection of the just (Luke 14:14) Beasts have bodily eyes to see the ordinary light of the day: but you endeavor with the eyes of faith, to foresee the glorious light of that day.

2. You know not how near, the evil spirit which night and day, like a roaring lion, walks about seeking to devour you (1 Pet 5:8; Job 1:7) was to you while you were asleep and not able to help yourself; and you know not what mischief he would have done to you, had not God hedged you and your with his ever-waking Providence, and guarded you with his holy and blessed angels (Job 1:10; Psalm 121:4; Psalm 34:7; Gen 32:1-2; 2 Kings 6:16)

3. If you hear the cock crow, remember Peter, to imitate him (Luke 22:61-62;) and call to mind that cock-crowing sound of the last trumpet, which shall waken you from the dead. And consider in what case you were, if it sounded now, and become such as you would then wish to be; lest at that day you should wish that you had never seen this; yes, curse the day of your natural birth, for lack of being newborn by spiritual grace (Jer 20:14; Job 3:1; Titus 3:5) When the cock crows the thief despairs of his hope, and gives over his night's enterprise: so the devil ceases to tempt, or attempt any further, when he hears the devout soul wakening herself with morning prayer.

4. Remember that Almighty God is about your bed, and sees your down-lying, and your uprising; understands your thoughts, and is acquainted with all your ways (Psalm 139:2-3) Remember likewise that his holy angels, who guarded and watched over you all night, does also behold how you wake and rise (Gen 31:55; Gen 32:1-2) Do all things, therefore, as in the solemn presence of God, and in the sight of his holy angels (Psalm 91:5, 11; Acts 12:11)

5. As you are putting on your apparel, remember that they were first given as coverings of shame, being the effects of sin; and that they are made but of the offals of dead beasts. Therefore, whether you respect the clothes, you have so little cause to be proud of them, that you have great cause to be humbled at the sight and wearing of them, seeing the richest apparel are but fine covers of shame. Meditate rather, that as your apparel serves to cover your

shame, and to fence your body from cold, so you should be as careful to cover your soul with that wedding garment which is the righteousness of Christ (because apprehended by our faith), called the righteousness of the saints (Matt 22:11; Rom 13:14; 1 Cor 1:30; Phil 3:9; Rev 19:8; Eph 4:24;) lest, while we are richly appareled in the sight of men, we be not found to walk naked (so that all our filthiness be seen) in the sight of God (Rev 16:15) But that with his righteousness, as with a robe, we may cover ourselves from perpetual shame; and shield our souls from that fiery cold that will procure eternal weeping, and gnashing of teeth (Matt 22:13) And withal consider how blessed a people were our nation, if every silken suit did cover a sanctified soul. And yet a man would think, that on whom God bestowed most of these outward blessings, of them he should receive greatest inward thanks (Luke 12:48) But if it proves otherwise, their reckoning will prove the heavier in the day of their accounts.

6. Consider how God's mercy is renewed unto you every morning, in giving you, as it were, a new life (Lam 3:23; Psalm 19:5), and in causing the sun, after his incessant race, to rise again to give you light. Let not, then, this glorious light burn in vain; but precede rather (as oft as you can) the sun rising to give God thanks (Luke 12:48;) and kneeling down at your bedside, salute him at the day-spring with some devout morning soliloquy: containing a humble confession of your sins, seeking the pardon of all your faults, a thanksgiving for all his benefits, and a craving of his gracious protection to his church, yourself, and all that belong to you.

CPSIA information can be obtained
at www.ICGtesting.com
Printed in the USA
FFOW01n1333090418
46216987-47527FF